AN INTRODUCTION TO ETHICS

MACMILLAN AND CO., Limited
LONDON · BOMBAY · CALCUTTA · MADRAS
MELBOURNE

THE MACMILLAN COMPANY
NEW YORK · BOSTON · CHICAGO
DALLAS · ATLANTA · SAN FRANCISCO

THE MACMILLAN COMPANY
OF CANADA, LIMITED
TORONTO

AN INTRODUCTION TO ETHICS

FOR TRAINING COLLEGES

BY

G. A. JOHNSTON, M.A., D.Phil.

LECTURER IN MORAL PHILOSOPHY IN THE UNIVERSITY OF GLASGOW
LECTURER IN ETHICS IN THE GLASGOW TRAINING COLLEGE

MACMILLAN AND CO., LIMITED
ST. MARTIN'S STREET, LONDON
1931

COPYRIGHT

First Edition 1915.
Reprinted 1920. 1924. 1931.

170
J72i

PRINTED IN GREAT BRITAIN

PREFACE

THIS little book is designed primarily for students in Training Colleges. In many of these Colleges Ethics is a "professional subject," and the students naturally expect that it will be treated in such a way as to reveal its bearing on the work which they will have to do in the education of the young. In this book it has been my aim to drive a few main lines through ethical theory, and to indicate the application of moral principles to the actual life of the school.

On three points a word of explanation may perhaps be necessary. In the attempt to secure simplicity and brevity, I have avoided, as far as possible, all controversial details, and have endeavoured to state principles positively and clearly. In doing this I have sometimes been forced to try to write more definitively than I should have ventured to do had I been addressing another audience. In a brief and elementary course of Ethics, hesitating qualification and negative criticism are apt to produce confusion in the mind of the student; and at the risk of seeming unduly dogmatic I have tried to reach positive and definite conclusions.

I have chosen to approach the problems of Ethics by way of Psychology; and that for two reasons. In the first place, Training College students have usually had some instruction in Psychology before taking a course in Ethics, and they enter on the latter study more naturally and easily if the psychological prolegomena are emphasised. Further, it is almost impossible to show the relation between Ethics and Moral Education, unless the psychological aspects of Ethics are constantly brought into prominence. On the other hand, the metaphysical foundation of Ethics has been kept strictly in the background. A metaphysical theory does underlie the general argument of these pages, but I have never obtruded it, because a Metaphysic that could be stated in a book such as this would clarify nothing, and might confuse much.

In dealing with the application of moral principles to the work of education, I have been content to indicate broad effects and general lines of influence. Nothing more than this could well be done in an introductory text-book of Ethics. But I have in preparation a small book on Moral Education, which will attempt to treat, in detail, of ways and means of moral instruction and moral training in schools.

It is a pleasure to acknowledge the debt which the book owes to Mr. J. C. Smith, H.M. Chief Inspector of Training Colleges, and to my colleagues, Mr. J. W. Scott and Mr. A. K. White, all of whom read the greater part of the manuscript and made many valuable suggestions.

G. A. JOHNSTON.

THE UNIVERSITY,
  GLASGOW, *July* 1915.

CONTENTS

CHAPTER   PAGE

I. INTRODUCTORY: ETHICS AND MORAL EDUCATION - - - - - 1

§ 1. What is Ethics? § 2. The Vocation of Man. § 3. Ethics and Moral Education. § 4. Plan of the Book.

PART I. THE GROUNDWORK OF CHARACTER

II. HEREDITY AND ENVIRONMENT - - 14

§ 1. Character, Heredity and Environment. § 2. Physical Heredity. § 3. The Principle of Stability. § 4. The Principle of Change. § 5. The Physical Environment. § 6. Mental and Moral Inheritance. § 7. The Social Environment. § 8. Moral Responsibility. § 9. Some Educational Aspects.

III. INSTINCTIVE BEHAVIOUR - - - 41

§ 1. What are Instincts? § 2. Some Prominent Human Instincts. § 3. The Social Significance of Instinct. § 4. The Education of Instinct. § 5. Instinctive Behaviour and Moral Conduct.

CONTENTS

CHAPTER		PAGE
IV.	IMPULSE AND DESIRE	57

§ 1. Impulse and Instinct.   § 2. The Control of Impulse.   § 3. Desire.   § 4. The Education of Desire.   § 5. Ambition, the System of Desire.

V. EMOTION AND SENTIMENT - - - 67

§ 1. The General Characteristics of Emotion.   § 2. The Control and Organisation of Emotion.   § 3. Sentiments.

VI. THE MORAL SELF - - - - 83

§ 1. The Growth of the Self.   § 2. The Social Nature of the Self.   § 3. Personality and Vocation.   § 4. The Self and its Habits.   § 5. Some Educational Aspects.

VII. WILL AND CONSCIENCE - - - 100

§ 1. The Self as Purposive and Regulative.   § 2. The Nature of Volition.   § 3. The Training of the Will.   § 4. Some Educational Aspects.   § 5. The Meaning of Conscience.   § 6. Conflicts of Conscience.   § 7. The Education of Conscience.

PART II. THE REALISATION OF CHARACTER IN VOCATION

VIII. CHARACTER AND CONDUCT - - 117

§ 1. The Growth of Character.   § 2. The Relation of Character to Conduct.   § 3. The Meaning of Conduct.   § 4. The Implications of Conduct: Freedom, Responsibility, Obligation and Value.   § 5. Conduct and the School.

CONTENTS

IX. THE STANDARD OF MORAL JUDGMENT — 127

§ 1. The Development of Moral Judgment. § 2. The Standard as Private Opinion. § 3. The Standard as Social Convention. § 4. The Standard as Feeling. § 5. The Standard as Reason.

X. THE MOTIVES AND SANCTIONS OF CONDUCT — 139

§ 1. Preliminary Remarks. § 2. Analysis of a Typical Moral Action. § 3. Is Motive or Consequence the Test of Right and Wrong? § 4. Why should I be Good? § 5. The Sanction of Punishment. § 6. The Sanction of Success. § 7. Criticism of the Sanctions. § 8. The Educational Value of External Sanctions.

XI. THE PLACE OF DUTY IN THE MORAL LIFE — 153

§ 1. Moral Obligation. § 2. Why is it Hard to do our Duty? § 3. Rules of Duty. § 4. The Authority of Duty. § 5. Duty and the Self.

XII. THE PLACE OF PLEASURE IN THE MORAL LIFE — 167

§ 1. Pleasure and Life. § 2. Hedonism. § 3. Utilitarianism. § 4. Is Pleasure the Moral Standard? § 5. Is Pleasure the Object of Desire? § 6. Pleasure and the Self.

CHAPTER		PAGE
XIII.	VOCATION	180

§ 1. Pleasure, Duty, and Happiness. § 2. The Choice of Vocation. § 3. Self-assertion and Self-repression. § 4. Loyalty to Vocation. § 5. Training for Vocation.

XIV.	GOODNESS AND THE VIRTUES	205

§ 1. The Struggle of the Moral Life. § 2. The Virtues, or Aspects of Goodness. § 3. Courage. § 4. Temperance. § 5. Justice. § 6. Wisdom. § 7. The Education of the Virtues.

XV.	THE INSTITUTIONS OF THE MORAL LIFE	220

§ 1. Morality and Social Institutions. § 2. The State. § 3. The Family. § 4. The School. § 5. The Church. § 6. Moral Progress and Optimism.

INDEX — 249

CHAPTER I.

INTRODUCTORY: ETHICS AND MORAL EDUCATION.

§ 1. **What is Ethics?** It is usual to enter on the study of any science by giving some definition of it. What, then, is ethics, and what is the subject-matter with which it deals? All sciences consist of answers to questions. The inquisitive child who wearies his mother with his questions is on the high-road to science. He wonders why the fire burns, why the wheels of the watch go round, what the moon is made of, and why his stomach hurts. To satisfy his wonder he asks questions. This is the attitude of the true scientist. Newton asked himself why the apple falls to the ground; and discovered, as the answer to the question, the law of gravitation.

When a science has been developed, it consists of a body of answers to a certain general question. Thus, the science of mathematics consists of a system of answers to the question, What is the nature of number and quantity? Astronomy is an attempt to answer the question, What are the laws which govern the planets and other celestial bodies? Physiology seeks to answer the question, What is the constitution of the human body?

Now, when we have before us the results of such sciences as these, when we know the answers they have given to their questions, a further question still remains to be asked. We must ask, What is the *value* of these answers ? What is the *good* of their results ? What is the value of the physiologist's researches ? What is the good of knowing the distance of the Earth from the Sun ? This kind of question with regard to the value or good of their investigations is not usually asked by the particular sciences themselves. Yet it is a question of fundamental importance.

This sort of question is one of the first that the child asks. The child is forward to ask, What is the good of this ? What is the good of that ? In its school-work it asks, What is the good of grammar, what is the good of decimals, what is the good of learning dates ? and so on. One of the child's stoutest objections is, " I don't see the good of it." The child is anxious to know the value of the actions he is made to do and the knowledge he is made to acquire. His questions are often disconcerting, and we find it difficult to give any satisfactory answer. " What's the good of going to Church ? " " What's the good of poetry ? " " What's the good of finding the South Pole ? "

> " ' But what good came of it at last ? '
> Quoth little Peterkin.
> ' Why, that I cannot tell,' said he."

The more complex civilisation grows, the more difficult it becomes to explain or to understand the good or value of the actions that men perform, the aims they set before themselves, and the knowledge that they acquire. In a simple and primitive community the good of every action can readily be explained. The South Sea Islander knows what is the good of fishing. It is to satisfy his hunger. He knows what is the good of climbing for milk-cocoa-nuts. It is to quench his thirst. He knows what is the good of sacrificing to the gods. It is that they may send rain, or protect him from his enemies. He knows what is the good of everything he does. All his actions have reference to human life. All his activities are directed to the preservation of his own life and those of his tribe. The good of his actions is their value-for-life.

It is easy for the savage to see what is the good of his actions, because his ends are limited and his aims are narrow. Almost all his actions are dictated by some primitive impulse or by a desire to obtain some fragmentary end. But in a complex civilisation, such as our own, the ends that men set before themselves may be very comprehensive and very remote ; and it is often extremely difficult to see the value of the actions they perform and the knowledge they acquire. Yet ultimately it will be found that all the aims of man, whether in the complicated society of a high civilisation, or in a primitive community of savages, have value only in relation to life. This is the ultimate good of all man's material and spiritual achievements, of all that he does and knows. The good of a thing is its value-for-life.

In many cases it may not be easy to see precisely what value-for-life a certain action possesses. What is the value-for-life of the discovery of the South

Pole ? It might be replied that Scott and Amundsen believed that the discovery of the Pole had a value-for-life because of the geographical, geological, and meteorological discoveries made by the Polar parties ; and, quite apart from the value of these researches, the example of unselfishness and sturdiness and heroism shown by the explorers had a real value-for-life for the rest of humanity. It may, of course, often happen that an action which seemed to the agent to have some value-for-life really has none. But a man always aims at what he believes will have some value-for-life.

We must beware of interpreting value-for-life in too narrow a way. What has value-for-life is not simply to be identified with what is useful. What is useful does have value-for-life ; but many things which are not useful also have value-for-life. Value-for-life is a more comprehensive term than usefulness, and includes much that is not useful. Music, art, and literature, for instance, are not useful in the ordinary sense of the word, but they certainly have great value-for-life.

Everything, then, that man does is done because it is conceived to have a value-for-life. And this is a value for *human* life. Every action and judgment has some relation to man, and has some reference to what is good for man. But what *is* the good for man ? If all action and all science have a value-for-life, there must be some good for man. The question what that good is is the question that ethics asks and tries to answer. What is the good of human life ? What is the aim of human life ? What is man's chief end ?

§ 2. **The Vocation of Man.** If we ask the plain man, What is the good for man? we shall receive very different answers. One man will answer that the aim of human life is the enjoyment of pleasure, another that it is the attainment of fame, another that it is the acquisition of knowledge, a fourth that man's chief end is, in the words of the Westminster Catechism, "to glorify God and to enjoy Him for ever." These answers are clearly very different, but if we examine them a little, we shall see that there is one thing that they all imply. They all involve a reference to man's character. Those who say that the great aim of life is the attainment of pleasure assume that pleasure is to be enjoyed by a person with a character of some stability. The very fact that a person has an aim at all, even though it be so low a one as the life of mere enjoyment, shows that he has some character. Only the man who is entirely aimless is totally devoid of character. Again, those who say that the end of life is the attainment of fame and honour certainly imply a reference to character. If they are sincere in their ambition, they desire not merely that honour should be ascribed to them, but that their characters should be such as to deserve the honour. They want to deserve it, for it is not real honour unless they deserve it. Honour is simply the outward recognition of the fact that there is something great and good about a man's character. Similarly, the other two views of the good for man both have reference to character. The acquisition of knowledge naturally has an influence, either good or bad, on the development of character; and the religious man knows that he cannot glorify God and enjoy Him unless his own character be good and his own conscience clear.

All these answers, then, different as they are, agree in implying that the good for man is intimately connected with his character. And we may state provisionally that the good for man consists in the development of a strong character in the activities of a socially valuable position in the community. All that this means will be explained fully in subsequent chapters: in particular, it will be shown (a) that this is the highest aim any man can have, and (b) that this aim is possible for every man.

Ethics, then, deals with the vocation of man and the character which he forms in fulfilling that vocation. The subject-matter of ethics is character and conduct. Now, we might have inferred this at once from the etymology of the name ethics. Ethics is derived from the Greek word ἦθος, which means formed character. Further, the word ἦθος is connected with ἔθος, which means custom or habit. Ethics is the science of character, the science which deals with moral customs and habits of conduct. Ethics is sometimes called moral philosophy, a name which is derived from the Latin *mores*, meaning primarily customs and habits, and secondarily the habits of moral agents in respect of moral action, *i.e.* character.

But ethics does not simply describe the various kinds of conduct and custom which we actually find among different races of men. It is not content to enumerate the moral customs of the world, and to state the kind of conduct that they sanction. Ethics

ETHICS AND MORAL EDUCATION 7

is always concerned with the rightness or wrongness of conduct : it deals with the character and conduct of man, in so far as it is good or bad, right or wrong. Ethics always approves or disapproves, it sets a value, negative or positive, upon conduct. It appraises and evaluates conduct. It reflects on conduct, and pronounces human actions good or bad, with reference to some standard or criterion.

§ 3. **Ethics and Moral Education.** Perhaps it may be asked, What is the good of ethics ? What is the use of reflecting on conduct ? Even a very little experience of the world shows us that the happiest and best people are often those who have reflected least on character and conduct. Goodness and happiness, like health, are things about which the ordinary man rarely thinks unless they are impaired. There are moments when we feel, like Hamlet, the misery of being able to reflect at all : our native resolution becomes all sicklied o'er with the pale cast of thought. At such times we are apt to sympathise with Voltaire's dictum, " Travaillons sans raisonner ; c'est le seul moyen de rendre la vie supportable." And it is true that people often speak grammatically without ever having studied grammar, argue logically with no knowledge of logic, keep perfect health in blissful ignorance of hygiene, and live good lives although they have never heard of ethics.

Yet in all these departments of life we believe in education. Man is a *rational* animal, and willy-nilly he must think. It is natural that he should reflect on his behaviour. The educator is aware, of course, that all men do not speak grammatically, or argue logically, or live healthily, or act rightly ; and he is convinced that in all these departments of life it is possible to use education with valuable results. Education maintains that in general the more a man knows about grammar, the more likely he is to correct his faults and learn to speak grammatically. Education holds that a knowledge of hygiene will sometimes save a man from disease, and will improve the general health of the community. So the moral educator believes that the more a man has reflected about conduct and character, the less likely he is to do wrong, and the more likely he is to do right.

But the success of all education depends on the willingness to improve of the person who is being educated. The educator can't *make* a child speak grammatically, unless the child *wants* to speak grammatically. He can't make the child argue logically, unless the child wants to argue logically. He can't make the child live healthily, unless the child wants to preserve his health. And he can't make the child act rightly, unless the child wants to act rightly. Nobody will benefit from education of any kind, unless he is willing to take advantage of it. Ethics will never make a man good. Grammar will never make him grammatical. Hygiene will never make him healthy. But if he wants to be healthy and good, he may learn much that will help him from hygiene and ethics.

It is the task of the moral educator to apply the principles of ethics, just as the physical instructor applies the principles of hygiene and physiology. As the physical instructor ought to know something about physiology and hygiene, so the moral educator ought to have some acquaintance with the principles of ethics. The moral educator ought to have, as one of his qualifications, some knowledge of the laws that govern the growth of character, the grounds on which our judgments of right and wrong ought to be based, and the great ends to which human life and work ought to be dedicated.

The opponents of moral education often expect far too much from it. They expect that it will *make* boys and girls better. And then they criticise it because this result frequently does not follow. As a French teacher has said, " My prizeman in morals is the biggest knave of the lot." [1] But there is nothing to be greatly surprised at in that. It simply means that that boy did not want to be good. And no amount of ethics will ever make him good, unless he wants to be good. In this respect moral education is in precisely the same position as education in general. No amount of grammar will make a boy grammatical, unless he wants to be grammatical.

Education in general sometimes seems to have better results than moral education. When that is so, the reason is this. Practically everybody *wants* to be able to speak grammatically, to read and write well, to count correctly, and to live a healthy life. But not everybody wants always to act rightly. *If* a person wants to be good, wants to act rightly, wants to do what he ought to do, then ethics may be of great value to him.

---

[1] *Moral Instruction and Training in Schools*, edited by M. E. Sadler, vol. ii. p. 23. In France ethics is taught as a " subject " in schools.

In addition to this, the moral educator may do something to inspire the child to want to act rightly. If he is brought into contact with the child young enough, while its character is still being formed, and the system of its wants and desires is still being developed, he may do much to influence it, to turn its desires in the right direction. Moral education may help the child to learn to want the right things. And that is of supreme importance. But moral education can never *make* a child good.[1]

§ 4. **Plan of the Book.** At this point, it seems worth while to anticipate for a moment, and to sketch, in the merest outline, the general argument of the book. This brief analysis is not, of course, completely self-explanatory; but it will perhaps be enough to indicate roughly the scope of our study, and the general lines on which we try to answer the question that Ethics asks. That answer, we have already suggested, may be provisionally phrased thus: " The good for man consists in the development of a strong character in the activities of a socially valuable position in the community." Now, in trying to understand all that this means, we must first trace the natural development of character, and examine in detail the various elements which go to constitute it. This is done in Part I. Then, in Part II., we consider the relation between

[1] The reader who is acquainted with works on ethics may be surprised that no attention has been paid to certain important questions with regard to the nature of ethics and its place among the sciences. I have considered it inadvisable to discuss these controversial questions in a book such as this; but I may perhaps be allowed to refer, for a statement of my views, to an article on "Ethics and Casuistry" in the *International Journal of Ethics*, July 1914.

character and conduct; examine the grounds on which conduct is regarded as right or wrong; and show how character is realised in actual conduct in performing the duties of a worthy station in the community.

At the beginning of Part I. we deal with the origin of character in the tendencies and capacities which the child inherits from his parents. But, if we say that the ultimate groundwork of character is provided by heredity, we must remember that, from the first, the tendencies and capacities which the child inherits are influenced by his physical and social environment (Chap. II.).

Next we consider the instincts with which the child starts life, and show how these are modified and developed to form the basis of the great institutions of the moral life (Chap. III.).

Then, along two main lines, we follow the development of character out of the instinctive origins of human behaviour.

First, we show that impulses, which may be regarded as instincts in their active or executive aspects, may be controlled and developed into desires, which are relatively permanent and pervade the whole of life (Chap. IV.).

Secondly, emotions, which in their origin appear at the instinctive level of human life, may be organised into sentiments, which have a profound influence on the evolution of conduct (Chap. V.).

But comprehensive as these sentiments and desires are, they may yet lead to conflict and disharmony in the moral life, unless they are unified in a permanent self. We accordingly have to examine the meaning of the self, and the importance of its habits. We have now reached the level of formed character (Chap. VI.).

Finally, we consider the self in two of the aspects of its relation to practical life, first as willing its actions, and then as judging its own and other people's thoughts and actions. The self in these two aspects is usually called will and conscience (Chap. VII.).

Throughout the whole of the first part, we are not content merely to trace the development of character. From point to point we suggest means whereby the teacher may seek to influence the growth of the child's character, when that shall seem advisable. The teacher may fairly hope to do something to help the child to desire the right things, to feel in the right way, and to form the right habits. In short, the child may be influenced to *want* to be good.

In Part II. it is assumed, for the most part, that the child *wants* to be good, and to do what is right. The great question is then asked, How is the child to *know* what is right and good ? Part II. comprises an attempt to answer that question.

First, we consider the relation of character and conduct, and investigate what precisely we mean by conduct. We find that when we speak of a man's conduct we imply that he is free to act, that he is responsible for his actions, that he has a moral obligation to act in certain ways, and that his actions have some moral value, positive or negative (Chap. VIII.).

We then go on to consider the grounds on which

we base our moral judgments, our judgments of the moral value of actions (Chap. IX.).

Then we ask whether the rightness and wrongness of actions depends on their motives or their consequences, and whether any general reasons can be given why we should do right actions and abstain from wrong ones (Chap. X.).

This leads to a recognition of the importance of duty, and a discussion of its place in the moral life (Chap. XI.).

Is duty inconsistent with pleasure ? What is the significance of pleasure in life ? (Chap. XII.).

We conclude that pleasure is not the only thing in life, nor is duty the only thing in life. They may come into conflict; but the good man will find that his pleasure consists in doing his duty in his own station in the community. Thus he realises his character, and fulfils his vocation (Chap. XIII.).

In the next chapter we consider the relation of character and vocation to the various virtues or types of goodness which we find realised in human actions (Chap. XIV.).

And in the last chapter we examine, in the light of character and vocation, the importance of the four great institutions of the moral life, the Family, the Church, the State, and the School (Chap. XV.).

For further reading : J. S. Mackenzie : *Manual of Ethics*, Introduction ; J. H. Muirhead : *Elements of Ethics*, bk. i. ; J. Dewey and J. H. Tufts : *Ethics*, ch. i.

PART I.

THE GROUNDWORK OF CHARACTER.

CHAPTER II.

HEREDITY AND ENVIRONMENT.

§ 1. Character, Heredity, and Environment. If we examine the groundwork of character, we shall find that at any stage in the child's development his character is what it is in virtue of (1) the original inheritance which he has received from his ancestors, and (2) the modifications and alterations produced in his original nature by the influence of environment. In some children the sinews of character may be due to the former factor rather than the latter; in others, the environment may have exercised the dominant influence. But in every case the two factors are necessarily involved. Character cannot be produced by heredity alone. The child is not supplied at birth with a ready-made character, which environment can do nothing to alter or modify. On the other hand, the infant's mind is not simply a piece of blank paper on which the environment can make any marks it pleases. Environment alone does not produce character. All character arises from the interaction of both heredity and environment.

But this is not all there is to say about character. Even in its earliest years the child does not submit to be passively moulded by these two great influences. The child is not simply a mass of clay at the mercy of Heredity and Environment, the two hands of the Potter. The child himself takes a hand in the process of making his character. He reacts on the formative influences to which he is subjected, and as his system of purposes grows and his will-power develops, he definitely, though at first unconsciously, undertakes the task of fashioning his own character. Thus the three great factors in character-building are heredity, environment, and will. These are all represented in the saying, "Some men are born great, some achieve greatness, some have greatness thrust upon them." "Some men are born great"—this emphasises the importance of heredity; "some have greatness thrust upon them"—here is the factor of environment; "some achieve greatness"—this involves the activity of the man's will. But we must guard against supposing that any man's character is produced solely by heredity, or solely by environment, or solely by will. The relative importance of the three factors varies in different people, but in the formation of every character each element has had some rôle to play.

In this chapter we shall consider the significance of heredity and environment in their relation to character.

§ 2. **Physical Heredity.** All character has a physical basis. Every child has a body, and without a body it could have no character. In studying the development of character, we must therefore first examine the meaning of physical heredity. Heredity has been defined as the genetic relation that binds one generation to another. The individual's inheritance includes all that he is, or has, to start with, in virtue of this genetic relation. The importance of heredity is recognised in phrases that have become household words. "A chip of the old block" suggests the essential continuity of one generation with those that preceded it; and "Blood will tell" illustrates the popular conviction that the past generation determines the development of the present.

What exactly is included in the inheritance? It has been represented pictorially by President D. S. Jordan as a "pack." In *The Heredity of Richard Roe*, President Jordan makes an analysis of the contents of the pack with which the typical individual Richard Roe starts life.[1] First of all, the pack contains the general characteristics of his common humanity, the general qualities that belong to him in virtue of the fact that he is a human being, and not a bird or a fish. In addition, the pack comprises the features which belong to the race of which he has been born a member. If he be of Celtic parentage, his pack will contain the characteristics of the Celtic stock. He will be fiery, but

[1] It must be remembered that this distinction between Richard Roe and his pack is largely figurative. At first, at least, Richard Roe and his pack are the same thing. The individual and his inheritance are, to begin with, one and the same.

not with the passion of the South Italian; he will be imaginative, but without the mental symbolism of the Oriental. But his pack includes also those more particular characteristics which he has inherited directly from his parents—peculiar features in which he resembles them, and which mark him off as *their* son. And lastly, the pack will contain some elements which it is impossible to assign to any determinate quarter. These characteristics will be found in his pack, and in his alone. They are the peculiarities and idiosyncrasies which belong to him alone, and which differentiate him from all other people, even from his parents and brothers.

The proportion of this comprehensive inheritance that is due to the various generations of the child's ancestors has been calculated; and may be stated most conveniently in the form in which it was formulated by Sir Francis Galton in his *Law of Ancestral Inheritance*. Galton showed that on the average in every inheritance the two parents together contribute one half, the grandparents between them one quarter, and so on in the regular series $\frac{1}{2} + \frac{1}{4} + \frac{1}{8} + \ldots$ This law holds good on the whole, but it gives no guidance in dealing with particular cases.

Heredity involves two aspects. "The hereditary relation is such that like tends to beget like, while at the same time opportunity is afforded for the individual new departures which we call variations. Both the tendency to persist and the tendency to diverge are included in the hereditary relation, so that it is confusing to make an absolute antithesis between heredity and variation. Heredity, seen in its fullest sense, is the larger concept, and includes both inertia and divergence, both continuance and change. Whatever be the terms used, there are two complemental facts : that like tends to beget like, yet that every new creature has in some way an individuality of its own." [1] Both these truths are illustrated by the fact of common experience that the child is like its parents in some respects, and differs from them in others.

§ 3. **The Principle of Stability.** The principle that like tends to beget like is responsible for the fundamental identity of humanity from one generation to another. The biologist explains why like tends to beget like by the theory of the "germ-plasm." The part that the germ-plasm plays in securing the similarity of one generation to the next has been well explained by Weismann. "In development," he says, "a part of the germ-plasm contained in the parent egg-cell is not used up for the construction of the body of the offspring, but is reserved unchanged for the formation of the germ-cells of the following generation." Certain germ-cells are specially set aside to perform the function of reproduction. These cells have not been exhausted in body-building, but have preserved intact the full inheritance which the individual has received, ready to be passed on to the succeeding generation. Thus, as Professor J. Arthur Thomson says, "The parent is rather the trustee of the germ-plasm than the producer of the child."

This undying germ-plasm supplies the principle of continuity from one generation to the next. It

[1] Thomson and Geddes : *Evolution*, p. 114.

HEREDITY AND ENVIRONMENT

guarantees the persistence of the same characteristics. It secures the stability of the race. The steadying influence of heredity has been corroborated by an abundance of statistics. The conservative tendency of heredity always works in the interest of mediocrity. It is constantly operating to bring men and women back to an average type. This may be illustrated from evidence with regard to height. It was found that fathers 72 inches in height had sons whose average height was 70·8 inches; while fathers 66 inches tall had sons with a mean height of 68·3 inches. In each case the average height of the sons showed a tendency to return to the normal. The fact to which this evidence bears witness is true of all human powers and capacities. The dominant tendency in heredity is for men to revert to the normal and average. What then has prevented heredity from reducing all mankind to the same dead level? The answer is found in the fact of variation.

§ 4. **The Principle of Change.** Variation, as we have seen, is simply one aspect of heredity. It is the tendency to diverge, as contrasted with the tendency to persist. Both tendencies spring from the same germ-plasm. The changes in individuals are really expressions of the vitality of the germ-plasm, just as their persistent similarity is. To the fact of variation is due the diversity of the world of life. No two living creatures are precisely alike. Every fir differs from its neighbour, and no two oak-leaves are exactly similar. Much greater are the differences between human beings, even though they be of the same family. Variation is responsible for all progress and all degeneration. No advance would be possible, if offspring had always exactly resembled their ancestors.

Variations are usually divided into two main kinds. Between these there are important differences.

(1) Some variations are inborn. Environment has had no influence in their production. They are inherent in the constitution of the individual, and belong to it at birth. These variations appear abruptly in the child. They cannot be accounted for by the habits or surroundings of the parents of the child in whom they make their appearance. Biologists call these variations discontinuous variations or "sports." They have collected much evidence to show that these discontinuous variations occur on a large scale among plants and animals. In human beings also there are instances. The child who is born with great musical abilities may be the son of parents quite devoid of them. Nearly every genius is a "sport" or discontinuous variation. When once discontinuous variations have occurred, they *may* be transmitted to offspring, and thus become a permanent heritage of the species.

(2) Other variations are acquired. They are not born with the child : the child acquires them during its life by interaction with its environment. They are developed by the child under some external stimulus, such as climate or injury. Thus they show the direct influence of the environment. If the child be brought up in a tropical country, he may acquire a sallowness that will last for life. Through injury he may lose the use of a limb.

The child may learn to speak French, may acquire a new nationality or religion, may take to drink, may learn to gamble and swear. All these new acquisitions are "acquired characters." Among biologists the question whether such acquired characters can be transmitted has aroused the keenest controversy. On the whole there is a balance of authority for the view that no convincing evidence of their transmission has yet been forthcoming. We shall assume, in what follows, that this biological view is correct, *i.e.* that acquired characters are not transmitted.

§ 5. **The Physical Environment.** The environment is in some way or other the cause, or at least the occasion, of all the acquired characters which the individual develops. But it is more than that. The living creature owes its continued existence to its environment. The physical environment includes air, earth, light, heat, water, food, climate, scenery, and so on. From this environment all living beings, including man, derive nourishment and warmth, and without it life and growth would be impossible.

The tremendous importance of the direct influence of the physical environment on living creatures is most clearly seen in the case of plants and animals. Two or three illustrative points may be mentioned. (*a*) In some cases the environment exercises a regularly recurrent influence, and the living creature simply falls into step with it. For example, some kinds of tropical acacia have been so influenced by the regular alternation of a twelve-hours day and night, that they uniformly respond to it by opening their leaves during the day and closing them during the night. Again, the brown stoat regularly becomes the white ermine during the winter months.

(b) Where the environment is not regular in its influence, the temporary alterations in the organism to which it leads may be simply adjustments of longer or shorter duration. "The warm-blooded bird or mammal can within limits adjust its heat-production and heat-loss so that the temperature of the body remains the same whether that of the environment rises or falls."[1]

(c) In some cases the environment may make a permanent and indelible impression on the living creature. A change in the environment, be it sudden or gradual, may occasion modifications in the organism which will remain with it as permanent acquisitions. A storm may blow a tree permanently out of shape, and a few years in the tropics may tan a man for life. In such cases the environment has led to the development by the individual of "acquired characters."

(d) Yet the importance of the environment should not be unduly magnified. We should not think of it as an iron fate. In most cases it does not actually *cause* changes. It only elicits and restrains. All it does is to afford the occasion on which the creature itself changes. Even in instances of "protective mimicry," where the influence of the environment is most immediately apparent, the environment only supplies the stimulus in response to which the organism changes itself. "A green frog, if he is not among green leaves, but amid dull, colourless

[1] Thomson and Geddes: *Evolution*, p. 194.

HEREDITY AND ENVIRONMENT

surroundings, ceases to be bright green, and becomes a sombre grey. Put him among foliage again, and his green soon returns. It cannot be said that the green foliage has *caused* his colour to change. It is more correct to say that he has the power of changing his colour to suit his environment. If the frog happens to be blind, no change of colour takes place ; so that it is by the help of the eye and the nervous system that the change is effected." [1] Thus, even the lower animals have some say in their development ; they are not absolutely at the mercy of their environment.

When we come to man, we find that his command over his environment is much more complete than that of the lower organisms. Plants have no power at all to change their environment. Animals can move from one environment to another, but they can do very little to alter their environment. In general they must simply adapt themselves to their surroundings. Man is superior to the lower animals in his capacity to adapt himself to his environment. He can live on the Equator or at the North Pole ; he can exist at sea-level or at an altitude of many thousand feet ; he can travel thousands of miles on land, on sea, in the air, and under the sea. And man is the only animal that is able on a large scale to adapt his environment to his own needs and uses. The Hollander makes his country by building dykes to shut out the sea. The Englishman makes the desert blossom like the rose by damming the Nile. Man makes his environment his slave.

[1] Headley : *Problems of Evolution*, p. 49.

§ 6. Mental and Moral Inheritance.

We have seen that physical qualities are inherited. Are mental and moral characteristics inherited in the same way? Does the child inherit his father's mental and moral qualities as he does his eyes and hair?

Much evidence has been collected to show that mental ability is transmitted from parent to offspring. In particular, Prof. Karl Pearson has gathered a large amount of material with regard to the transmission of mental characteristics. School teachers in London were asked to report on such characteristics in their scholars as popularity, vivacity, ability, and handwriting. Information was collected with regard to the resemblance of the scholars to their parents in these respects; and as a result of the whole enquiry, Prof. Pearson maintained that "the degree of resemblance of the physical and mental characters of children is one and the same." Or, to put it otherwise, "We inherit our parents' temper, our parents' conscientiousness, shyness, and ability, as we inherit their stature, forearm, and span."[1]

Similar investigations have been made with regard to the transmission of moral characteristics. One of the most interesting of these studies is Dugdale's account of the "Jukes." Dugdale traces the history of some 1200 "Jukes," all descendants of a ne'er-do-weel who flourished about 1750 on the Hudson River. His descendants showed nothing but ignorance, idleness, and crime, combined with extraordinary fertility. The great majority of

[1] *Huxley Lecture for* 1903.

HEREDITY AND ENVIRONMENT

them, traced through seven generations, were criminals and paupers. Of the total number of men, less than 20 were skilled workmen, and of these 10 learned their trades in the State prisons. But it is not only the pure black strain that persists in this way. A study of the descendants of Jonathan Edwards shows that of the 1400 of them with regard to whom information was available, not a single one was a criminal or pauper, while the family had adorned every department of learning and activity in the United States.

These and similar studies make perfectly clear the remarkable persistence of mental and moral characteristics from one generation to the next. There can be no doubt that they do persist. But the real question is, Are these characteristics really inherited ? On the whole it seems probable that precise mental and moral qualities are not inherited like physical characteristics. Because certain mental and moral characteristics persist from one generation to another, it does not follow that they are inherited. They may simply be developed anew in each generation under the influence of the early environment. The "Jukes" all grew up in unfavourable environments, while the members of the Edwards family all enjoyed good surroundings in their early days. In most cases it is to the influence of the early home environment rather than to that of heredity that the persistence of precise mental and moral characteristics should be ascribed.

Yet it is certain that we can and do inherit *tendencies* and *capacities* in the mental and moral realm. We inherit, for instance, instincts, the forms of nervous mechanism which enable us to act usefully without having learned. We inherit temperaments and dispositions, which define our general emotional and practical attitude to the world. Most important of all, we inherit capacities, and our capacities include all that we are capable of becoming in intellect, in morality, in art, and in religion. What we inherit is not specific ability but general capacity. The son of a woman who is strong intellectually or morally may not be strong in exactly the same way as his mother, but he is likely to be strong in *some* way. The son of a great mathematician may not be a great mathematician, but his general mental capacities will probably be above the average. The child does not inherit the special ability or peculiar virtue of his parents, but he does inherit general capacities and general tendencies, which may express themselves in one way or another. The way in which they develop is determined by environment and training.

The capacities which we inherit form a limit beyond which we cannot advance. In the physical realm the limit of capacity is readily recognised ; and our physical heredity sets up absolute barriers beyond which we cannot pass. It is equally true that the extent of our mental acquisitions is limited by our inherited intellectual capacities. The teacher cannot make a first-class mathematician out of a child whose inherited capacity is mediocre. But we are usually far too apt to suppose that we have reached the limit of our mental capacities long before we really have. Most people regularly live

HEREDITY AND ENVIRONMENT 27

very much nearer the limits of their physical strength than they ever approach those of their mental powers.

In the moral realm we practically never reach the limit of our capacity for good and evil. Every child is born with unlimited potentialities either for good or for evil. But he inherits no fixed endowment of goodness, and he bears no burden of original sin. Capacities and tendencies are what he inherits. If his parents have been vicious, their sins will be transmitted to him, not as a complete second edition of their vice, but as a general weakness towards it. The virtues of his parents are transmitted to him, not as specific virtues, but as general health of mind and power of resistance to evil. His actual moral life, his thoughts and deeds, his convictions and habits, are of his own acquisition. All his morality is attained and achieved. Conduct is not inherited ; it is self-consciously made. Capacity is an inheritance, character is not an inheritance but an acquisition.

§ 7. **The Social Environment.** Character is acquired by the child through interaction with his environment. Environment means more to the child than to any other creature. The child's relation to his environment is a growing relation. And the child is the only animal that has a social environment. Great as is the influence of the physical environment, that of the social is much more profound and extensive. The presence and significance of this environment of moral and intellectual forces is not yet fully recognised. For it is not an environment which we can see or touch.

We can indeed point to some of its manifestations in ideas and ideals embodied in prose and verse, in music and painting, in Church and College, and, above all, in society itself. But we cannot measure it or tabulate it. Yet it means more to us than any other. From the child's earliest hours its influences have been playing upon him. It is present always, and counts because of its constant pressure. But because its relation to us is so intimate, and because it has so informed the very structure of our minds, we do not usually distinguish its influence upon us from the activities which we suppose we originate ourselves. In fact, we do not think about it at all, and if "environment" happens to be mentioned, our thoughts fly immediately to the physical world.

There is none of our experience which is not permeated by the social environment. From his environment the child derives the language he speaks. All his manners and customs are accepted from it without question and without reflection. His political opinions and religious beliefs have been largely supplied to him by it. His mental and moral life consists largely of opinions which he has accepted on the authority of the society in which he lives. He simply takes for granted the validity of his beliefs and customs. He takes them to be as fixed and certain as the rising and setting of the sun.

But there come times in the life of every individual when the traditions in which he has been brought up appear no longer adequate. The orthodox explanations of science and politics and religion no longer satisfy. Doubt has seized hold of his

HEREDITY AND ENVIRONMENT 29

mind. He determines to prove all things for himself on the touchstone of his own sagacity. Sometimes a whole community begins to question the authority of its manners and customs, its laws and institutions. Some great national perplexity arises, and the old ways of life are proved insufficient. The gradual growth and the slow progress of moralisation begin to suggest that the old beliefs are inadequate and the old customs unworthy. But even when the individual criticises his environment most severely, he criticises it because he is its own child. The society really uses him to criticise itself. The great reformer is always a thorough child of his time. It is precisely because his environment has saturated him so completely that he turns upon it in criticism.

It follows that environment is potent to counteract or encourage the hereditary tendencies which every child possesses, and whose persistence has been already illustrated. We all know how influential the environment is in corrupting good tendencies. It is a hackneyed commonplace, yet an unhappy truth, that the environment of the slum slowly but surely weakens the mental and moral strength of nearly all who enter it. Perhaps our thoughts are apt to dwell too much on this drab aspect of the operation of environment. But on the other side of the shield we have a brighter picture, and one that is no less true. Environment can exert a mighty power in restraining and repressing evil proclivities, and eliciting and confirming tendencies to good. "The records of charitable societies show that about 85 per cent. of the children of paupers and criminals who are placed in good homes at an early age become good citizens." [1]

Our attitude to our social environment is a double one. (*a*) On the one hand our attitude is receptive. There is little that we possess which we have not received from our environment. Our dependence on it is so complete, that apart from it we should be incapable of any rational or moral activity. The material of most of our mental and moral acquisitions is derived from it. (*b*) But we are not merely passive creatures, absolutely at the mercy of our environment. Our attitude to it is also re-creative. All the material which the environment supplies, whether that material be physical or spiritual, must be re-made, transmuted, and re-created before it can become a permanent possession of the soul. Just as the tree assimilates and transforms all the material which it receives from its environment, so the individual elaborates and re-creates all the endowments which his environment so lavishly bestows on him.[2]

§ 8. **Moral Responsibility.** How far is our frank recognition of the importance of environment and heredity compatible with moral responsibility? Is it not the case, it may be said, that you have ascribed half of man's character to heredity and the other half to environment? If that be so, what right have you to hold that man is responsible for his character and conduct? Does not moral responsibility vanish?

---

[1] Kirkpatrick: *Fundamentals of Child Study*, p. 299.

[2] This section owes much to the lectures and writings of Sir Henry Jones.

HEREDITY AND ENVIRONMENT

There is no reason why we should give up our belief in moral responsibility. We do recognise the tremendous importance of heredity and environment. But we should not think of them as if it were possible to portion out character between them. We should avoid thinking of environment and heredity as if each excluded the other. It is not true that the more we attribute to environment the less must we ascribe to heredity, and *vice versa*. Life and character imply their interaction. When the influence of the one increases, it does not follow that the influence of the other must decrease. On the contrary, the richer the inheritance with which the child starts, the greater the influence the environment may exert. The inheritance of the limpet or whelk is meagre. If a Bible be introduced into its environment, it will be able to make no use of it. But a Bible in the environment of a man may lead him to change the whole course of his life. Yet, however potent the influence of heredity and environment in their interaction, they do not absolutely determine the child's life and conduct. Character, as we shall see more fully in a subsequent chapter, is the product of will. The child gradually makes his own character. It is his own; he and he alone is responsible for it.

Environment will not absolve a man of responsibility for his actions. Environment may provide temptations and difficulties, or strengthening associations and friendships; but from the moral standpoint all that this means is that it is supplying the instruments with which the individual himself will carry out the process of character-building. The child's environment exists to be used, and as he grows up he more and more acquires the power of reacting upon it. Whether he makes a good or bad use of it depends ultimately on him alone. Parent or teacher or friend may point out how it should be used, what elements in it should be assimilated, and what avoided, but in the end the responsibility for choosing the right or the wrong rests with the individual himself. It is the privilege and prerogative of man to be, so far as his character is concerned, a creature of his own making.

But, it may be objected, if no acquired characters are transmitted, if all that we gain in toil and pain during our lives is doomed to perish with us, is not our responsibility a purely personal and private matter ? Our mental and moral acquisitions, it may be argued, have no significance for the race, because they cannot be transmitted to our offspring. Does this not remove the chief incentive to responsibility ? No, it does not ; and that for three reasons.

(1) With the denial of the transmission of acquired characters our sense of our personal responsibility for our actions is increased. We cannot blame a previous generation for our shortcomings. In the physical realm, indeed, the results of vice may be perpetuated ; but the child of the most dissolute parents may acquire moral strength. So far as morality goes, every child starts life with a clean, or almost clean, slate. Proclivities to good and evil it does indeed inherit ; and it is one of the great privileges of the educator to be always on the look-out for proclivities to encourage, or to restrain. But these are merely tendencies. In

HEREDITY AND ENVIRONMENT

some cases they may, indeed, be very strong, and may greatly further or retard the child's moral progress. But they do not absolutely determine the child's character. Heredity is no inscrutable fate to destroy the child's moral strength before he has begun to use it. We are masters of our own destiny; our deeds are really our own; and we alone are responsible for them.

(2) But our responsibility for our actions does not end with ourselves.[1] Our actions do not terminate in themselves. They form part of our neighbour's social environment, and may exert a profound influence upon him. Hence the sphere of our responsibility is far wider than the immediate consequences of our deeds. Every individual's character and conduct constitute a portion of his neighbour's social environment. Example is better than precept, and there is no greater influence for good on the community than the upright man. Trite as this is, it is a peculiarly sobering reflection for all engaged in education, and especially in elementary education. For hours of every day the teacher's words and deeds and manners form a most important part of the child's environment. Every action of the teacher is viewed by the child under the microscope of the class-room. Throughout the most impressionable and receptive years of the child's life, the teacher's character is one of the chief formative influences to which it is exposed.

(3) Our responsibility also extends, at least to

[1] " Our deeds are like children that are born to us: they live and act apart from our being " (George Eliot).

some extent, to posterity. For, though the next generation will not inherit specific virtues and special abilities, it certainly will inherit general capacities. Our mental and moral qualities may be inherited by the next generation as tendencies and proclivities. Now, as we have already seen, our characters are not absolutely determined by the tendencies we inherit, and of course it is also true that the tendencies inherited from us by our offspring will not inevitably and irrevocably fix their characters. But just as we were helped in the moral struggle by inherited tendencies to good and handicapped by inherited tendencies to evil, so the next generation will be assisted or retarded in the task of the making of character by the kind of tendencies they inherit from us. Thus, though we cannot transmit our acquired characters as such, we have a real responsibility towards posterity. The more diligent and conscientious the present generation is in developing special abilities and specific virtues, the higher is likely to be the general level of ability and uprightness in the next.

§ 9. **Some Educational Aspects of Heredity and Environment.** The influences of education form part of the social environment of the child. The power of the social environment in general has already been emphasised. In education this power is focussed and concentrated. The present age is little likely to under-estimate the value and effect of education. With immeasurably fuller knowledge of the meaning of heredity and environment than Locke had, it is able to echo his statement: "I think I may say that of all the men we meet with nine parts of ten are what they are, good or evil, useful or not, by their education. 'Tis that which makes the great difference in mankind." [1]

But we must recognise that the influence of education is limited in two respects. (*a*) As we have seen, there is no convincing evidence that the individual transmits to his offspring the special qualities which he has himself acquired during his life. Therefore, from the standpoint of heredity, the influence of education is very largely confined to the individual. None of the special virtues or specific abilities which he acquires will be perpetuated in the race.[2] On the other hand, it is an inspiration to the teacher to know that the child whom he has to train is never hopelessly corrupted by the acquired vices of his parents. (*b*) Again, the influence of education may be limited by the other forces which, along with it, constitute the social environment. The teacher may indeed manipulate the rest of the environment to some extent; but he can rarely secure that the environment as a whole will second his aims. The unfavourable environment of home and companions may counteract all his efforts.

Yet, in spite of these limitations, the dynamic influence of education can hardly be over-estimated. It is the teacher's duty and privilege to utilise all the help that heredity and environment can give.

(1) It will add to the fascination, as well as to the usefulness, of teaching to study the heredity

[1] *Some Thoughts Concerning Education*, par. 1.
[2] But cf. *supra*, p. 34.

of the individual child. To do this, it is necessary to know something of the child's parents. In the rural school this is quite possible, and the excellence of the results obtained by the old educational system of rural Scotland was largely due to the intimacy of the relation which usually existed between the village dominie and the parents of his pupils. In the city school it is rarely possible, except in isolated instances, for the teacher to meet his pupils' parents. In some kindergarten schools opportunities are provided for teachers and parents to meet. This experiment might usefully be extended to all elementary schools.[1] Regular social evenings might be promoted by the school, to which parents would be invited, and thus have an opportunity of meeting their children's teachers.[2] If one looks at the matter sanely, it is one of the most absurd things in the world that parents and teachers, the two groups which have the most profound influence on the development of the child's character, should work in entire ignorance of one another's aims and aspirations for the children.

But under present conditions the teacher must usually be content to study the child alone. He should certainly do this. As education becomes more and more systematised, there is great danger that an artificially mechanical scheme may ignore the individual differences between children. The teacher must seek to counteract one of the necessary

[1] Many schools have "Parents' Days," on which the parents may come and see their children at work.

[2] This is already done in many schools. See *Moral Instruction and Training in Schools*, edited by M. E. Sadler, p. 121.

evils of system by trying to understand the individual child, and by helping it to develop in accordance with its own individuality towards the fullest realisation of its capabilities. If he understands the child, he may be able to arouse dormant hereditary capacities, to repress tendencies to evil as they emerge, and to encourage and confirm the strong and well-balanced powers which promise most for the child's personal welfare and social influence.

(2) The teacher himself, as we have seen, forms a most important part of the child's social environment. He may use that environment, including himself, for the purposes of education in three ways.

(*a*) He can use the environment by way of *exemplification*. Nothing has so much influence over children, and especially young children, as an example to be followed. The example appeals to the child's primitive tendency to imitate. The teacher may utilise this tendency to imitation, by occasionally, *e.g.* during the History lesson or the Scripture lesson, drawing the attention of the children to examples that are worth imitating.

(*b*) The environment may be used to shape character by way of *suggestion*. This mode of influence is so quiet and pervasive that we rarely think about it, and perhaps for that very reason it is all the more potent in effecting its results. Nothing conduces more to the formation of good reading habits in a community than the institution of an attractive library, so arranged as to suggest in every detail the pleasures of reading. So, to influence the growth of the religious spirit, churches should breathe an atmosphere suggestive of the divine presence. Similarly, if the children are to make the most of their school-life, the subtle suggestion must be conveyed to them that it is pleasant. With a view to this, the teacher may seek to make the class-room as pleasant a place as possible, *e.g.* with flowers and pictures. For some reason the word "suggestive" has come to mean "suggestive of evil." Thus we speak of a "suggestive situation" or "suggestive action" or "suggestive novel" or "suggestive play." But we should remember that actions may be suggestive of good quite as directly and distinctly as they suggest evil.

(*c*) But suggestion will not do everything. Education must also utilise the environment by way of direct *instruction*. Instruction must always be the chief method of the educator, for it alone is definite and systematic. In giving moral instruction there are three things the teacher should bear constantly in mind. It is necessary to be positive. Negative precepts have much less power behind them than positive principles. The fundamental characteristic of the child is his activity. Hence the importance of telling him what to do rather than merely what to avoid. Again, the importance of the environment of Nature should be emphasised. The children should be encouraged to take every opportunity to understand the lessons of Nature, that they may assimilate her teaching, and become like her, constant, true, quiet, and strong. Lastly, the teacher should emphasise the value of associating with the best. Most children are naturally sociable; they do not require to be told to associate with one another; but they do need to be told to choose the best of their companions to be their friends. And in this connection reference may also be made to that companionship with the best minds and hearts of the world, which we may enjoy in reading.

In all these and in many other ways the teacher may seek to select the elements in the child's environment which will be most beneficial to his character, and, by a study of the child's hereditary tendencies, direct those influences into the channels where they will be most potent for good. But before ending this chapter, two words of warning must be dropped. Human nature, and especially child nature, is, like the Mary of the nursery rhyme, " quite contrary." The child is very apt to want to do things precisely because he is told not to, and to be disinclined to do them precisely because he is bidden to do them. This fact has always to be borne in mind when giving moral instruction. It is one reason why with some children the indirect influences of suggestion and example are more effective than direct moral instruction. This is where the teacher's study of the individual child will be invaluable. The second point is this. It is right that the teacher should magnify his office. But he should beware of thinking that he is " making " or " building " the child's character for it. That he cannot do. The teacher may in a multitude of ways give advice, warning, and encouragement, and thus may exert a quite incalculable influence on the development of the child's character; but in the last resort it is the child himself who makes his own character. And from the first the sense of responsibility should be laid upon the child.

For further reading : J. A. Thomson and P. Geddes : *Evolution*, ch. iv. and vi. ; J. A. Thomson : *Heredity*, ch. i., iii., vii., xiv. ; H. H. Horne : *Idealism in Education*, ch. ii. and iii.

CHAPTER III.

INSTINCTIVE BEHAVIOUR.

The basis of human character is to be found in instinctive behaviour. Long before the child is capable of forming definite purposes and consciously willing its conduct, it acts instinctively. Instinctive behaviour is specially characteristic of the child's early months; but the child does not drop its instincts with its baby-socks and bib. Human instincts are important, because they are capable of modification and development, and thus continue to form an integral part of conduct, even at its highest levels. Many of man's highest ideals are firmly rooted in primitive instincts, and his noblest institutions have their foundation in his instinctive behaviour.

But we should beware of thinking that because it can be shown that our ideals and aspirations are very closely related to primitive instincts they are therefore any the less lofty and noble. The ideal of motherhood is none the less sacred because it is grounded upon natural instincts, nor is the church any the less spiritual an institution because its appeal is based upon instincts which man shares with the brutes. If man's noblest aspirations have grown out of instinctive wants, and his highest institutions have been formed in response to persistent instinctive needs, the proper conclusion to be drawn is, not that these ideals and associations are, after all, mean and poor, but that the instincts from which they have developed are themselves valuable and worthy.

It is of importance, then, in tracing the development of character, to ask, What are instincts, How do they contribute to the formation of man's ideals and institutions, and How may they be educated?

§ 1. **What are Instincts?** In ordinary conversation we frequently speak of instincts. We refer to the animal's instinct of self-preservation, and the child's instinctive trustfulness. We say that this man has an instinct for friendship, and that one an instinct for religion. We speak of our instinctive liking for a new acquaintance. What we seem to mean by instinct in common parlance is simply something that is there to start with which we cannot explain. An instinctive mode of behaviour is a way in which a child naturally acts. An instinct is not artificial; it cannot be made. Something like this is the meaning which the man in the street attaches to instinct. On the whole, it is quite right; but it requires to be defined a little more precisely.[1]

Instincts are certainly inherited. They form part

---

[1] Instinct has been defined by Prof. Lloyd Morgan as "that which is on its first occurrence independent of prior experience; which tends to the well-being and preservation of the race, which is similarly performed by all the members of the same more or less restricted group of animals, and which may be subject to subsequent modification under the guidance of experience."

INSTINCTIVE BEHAVIOUR

of the congenital endowment with which the child starts life. In their origin they are not influenced by the child's experience. They belong to the child before he has acquired any experience at all. It is characteristic of what is instinctive that it does not require to be learnt. Instincts are usually *general*, and common to all members of the same group. Some instincts, *e.g.* that of self-preservation, seem to be common to all living creatures. Others are common only to particular species. Instinctive modes of behaviour are general : we do not inherit special ways of acting.

It is often difficult to distinguish instincts from what the psychologist calls reflex actions. But there are two main lines of distinction. (1) Reflex actions always occur in a fixed and regular way in response to an external stimulus. They occur only when the stimulus is present, and when it is present they occur naturally and necessarily. Thus, when a bit of dust flies into the eye, certain movements of the eyelids take place which tend to get rid of the intrusive speck. Instinctive behaviour, on the other hand, does not need a definite *stimulus* to elicit it. It is excited as a way of dealing with a relatively complex situation. (2) Reflex actions are fixed and uniform. For the most part they are incapable of modification. We cannot modify the reflex changes which take place in the pupil of the eye in response to changes in the intensity of the light. To put it briefly, while instincts are adaptive and modifiable, reflex movements are not.

Instincts may be adapted to the environment, in order to secure the well-being of the individual and the preservation of the race. They are subject to variation, and as experience grows they may be modified. Instincts contribute to the formation of experience, and in turn experience influences them. Most so-called instincts are not pure instincts. Even in the lower animals experience alters and improves instincts. Thus, chicks run and swim and dive and peck and scratch instinctively. They do not need to be taught to do any of these things. But experience may modify these instincts in special ways. "The inherited tendency of the chicks is to peck—to peck ' at anything and everything not too large.' But experience very rapidly teaches that it is pleasant to peck at some things, such as yolk of egg or cabbage-moth caterpillars, and very unpleasant to peck at others, such as cinnabar caterpillars or bits of orange peel. The tendency to peck at the one sort of object is accordingly confirmed. The tendency to peck at others is inhibited. . . . The instinctive tendency is regulated, narrowed, and defined, as it becomes a habit in which experience has played its part."[1]

§ 2. **Some Prominent Human Instincts.** If we take instinct in a narrow sense, to include only those modes of behaviour which occur in a fixed and uniform way at or near the beginning of infant life, our list of human instincts will be very short. The child instinctively clasps anything placed in its hand, it instinctively sucks the breast, and instinctively crawls. The infant also expresses itself instinctively by making vocal sounds and by smiling and frowning. But if we extend the

[1] Hobhouse : *Mind in Evolution*, p. 87.

term, in accordance with our use of it in the previous paragraph, to include modes of behaviour in which some element of experience may be included, our list grows very much longer. Some writers have enumerated over thirty human instincts. It will be enough for our purpose to consider a few of the most important.

(1) One of the earliest forms of instinctive behaviour is that prompted by fear. In its earliest hours the infant displays fear on the occurrence of any loud noise, and instinctively shrinks from it. This *shrinking* may develop into movements of flight and concealment as soon as the infant is capable of them. Along with this we may take the instinct of repulsion. The child instinctively shrinks from slimy creatures.

(2) The child instinctively opposes anything which rouses its anger. Any prolonged discomfort, or the interruption or lateness of a meal, will make the child angry. At first the infant has to be content to express its anger in cries; but, as soon as it is able, its instinctive opposition to what has aroused its anger issues in active *pugnacity*. "Many a little boy has, without any example or suggestion, suddenly taken to running with open mouth to bite the person who has angered him. . . . As the child grows up . . . and the means we take to overcome obstructions to our efforts become more refined and complex, this instinct ceases to express itself in its crude natural manner, save when most intensely excited, and becomes rather a source of increased energy of action."[1]

[1] M'Dougall: *Social Psychology*, p. 61.

(3) The instinct of *curiosity* appears a little later in the life of the child than those which we have considered. The child's interest is excited by objects which are novel to it, but they must not be so strange as to startle it. The instinct of curiosity expresses itself first in the roving of the eyes, and later in the attempt to grasp the strange object with the hands.

(4) The closely-related instincts of *self-assertion* and *self-abasement* are exhibited by the child in its relations with other people, and especially with other children of about its own age. It is apt to "show off," "put on side," swagger and brag—tendencies in which it is often encouraged by the applause with which parents and friends greet its early efforts to talk and walk. These displays of self-assertiveness often alternate with fits of shyness and bashfulness, which result immediately from the instinct of self-abasement.

(5) The *gregarious* instinct also appears early in the life of the child. The child's instinct for friendship is a special form of this instinct. The baby's smile seems to welcome everybody, and at a later stage children naturally herd together for their games.

(6) The instinct of *acquisitiveness* is not long in making its appearance in the normal child. Nearly every child makes a collection of something—stamps, postcards, cigarette photos, scraps, "paper people," birds' eggs, or any of a hundred and one other things, usually simply for the pleasure of collecting and without any definite purpose.

(7) For obvious reasons, the instinct of *sex* does not emerge until the child has reached the adolescent

stage, though premonitions of it may occur in very young children.

(8) The *parental* instinct is also late in making its appearance. But it is certainly anticipated in the maternal affection of the little girl for her dolls.

With regard to instincts in general, two things should be remembered. First, the possession of a multitude of *modified and modifiable* instincts is a mark of distinction between man and the lower animals. The instincts of the lower animals are much more fixed than those of man. Man's instincts are essentially amenable to training; and on this fact depends the possibility of human progress. Again, it should be noted that, as the acquired element is so prominent in human instincts, they vary in their strength and in the manner of their appearance. Human instincts differ greatly from individual to individual both in their nature and in their operation. To use Prof. Stout's illustration, falling in love is instinctive, but we do not all fall in love with the same readiness or the same intensity—or with the same kind of person.

§ 3. **The Social Significance of Instinct.** The instincts which have been mentioned form the foundation on which all moral and social life is based. Some of them are more directly social in their reference than others, but all have some social and moral importance. From the social standpoint it is convenient to consider the instincts, which we have just enumerated, in pairs.

First we take the reproductive and parental instincts. Their importance for society needs no emphasis. It is obvious that if the sexual instinct could be abolished, society would soon disappear altogether. In human beings the parental instinct is conjoined with the reproductive, and so closely are they correlated, that "in the individuals in whom one of them is strong the other will also be strong in the majority of cases, and *vice versa*."[1] The combination of these instincts results in the institution of the family; and there can be no doubt that the stability and integrity of the family is the *sine qua non* of the health of society. From these instincts directly spring some of the highest moral virtues. Self-sacrifice, along with a host of attendant virtues, is an immediate product of the instinct of parenthood; and "it is probable that these two instincts in conjunction, the reproductive and parental instincts, directly impel human beings to a greater sum of activity, effort, and toil, than all the other motives of human action taken together."[2] These instincts are specially the foundation of the Home.

The instincts of pugnacity and gregariousness also have an important social reference; and, different as they seem at first sight, they yet contribute in almost equal measure to the foundation of communities. Man is naturally the most gregarious of animals. "To be alone is one of the greatest of evils for him. Solitary confinement is by many regarded as a mode of torture too cruel and unnatural for civilised countries to adopt. To one long pent up on a desert island the sight of a human footprint or a human form in the distance would be the most tumultuously exciting of experiences."[3] To the

[1] M'Dougall: *Social Psychology*, p. 267. [2] *Ibid.* p. 269.
[3] James: *Principles of Psychology*.

gregarious instinct is due the fact that primitive men originally drew together into hordes, which gradually became more and more systematically organised. The gregarious instinct not only brings men into communities, but by its persistence it keeps them welded in these communities. To this result the instinct of pugnacity has also contributed. It would seem at first sight that if gregariousness is the instinct of unity, pugnacity is the instinct of diversity. It would seem that this instinct would keep men from mixing with their fellows. But the pugnacious instinct, which does originally raise every man's hand against his neighbour, is trained to hold itself in reserve to be used not against fellow-citizens, but against the public enemies of the State to which they belong. For the sake of protection, and in order to get the better of their enemies, men unite in communities, and direct their pugnacious instincts into wars on behalf of the community to which they belong. Thus both the origin and the continuance of settled communities depend on this instinct. And the two instincts in conjunction may be said to be the foundation of the State.

Another pair of instincts which may be considered together in their social significance are self-abasement and self-assertion on the one hand, and the instinct of shrinking and repulsion on the other. Man, in his early development, whether in the individual or the race, instinctively fears what he does not understand. Primitive man wonders at all he sees, and the combination of fear and wonder gives rise to respect and awe when he compares his own weakness with the strength of the mighty powers whose mysterious influence he cannot understand. The instinct of self-abasement is closely connected with man's veneration for superior powers. In contrast with them man minimises his own importance. As a result of the operation of these instincts, man gradually develops a mass of customary observance, with which he surrounds the objects of his veneration. These two instincts have contributed to the development of religion in the widest sense. In all primitive communities religious custom and observance has exercised a strongly conservative influence. Customary observance, buttressed by the sanctions of religion, has supplied the element of stability specially necessary to primitive society. These primitive religious instincts have persisted, and continue to play their part in all developed religions, though they have been moulded by the mellowing influences of such emotions as gratitude and love. Yet these two instincts form the basis of the Church.

The only other instincts whose social importance we need to consider are those of curiosity and acquisitiveness. The acquisitive instinct supplies one of the prime conditions of social progress. A people in whom this instinct is weak will make no progress. There still are in existence tribes of people who support themselves by hunting and collecting wild roots and fruits, and who have no homes and no possessions apart from what they can carry with them on their backs and in their hands. Modern civilisation depends on the fact that mankind has acquired a vast amount of possessions that are not required for the satisfaction of present needs, and which therefore form the great reservoir of capital with which modern industry is supplied. This instinct of acquisitiveness has also led to the acquisition of knowledge. All science depends on the operation of the instinct in forming the desire to add to the stock of human knowledge. The connection of this with the instinct of curiosity is obviously close. Man's speculative tendencies have their root in this instinct. Curiosity is one of the most distinctive characteristics of the child. We all know how persistently and importunately curious little children are. Toddy's curiosity to " see the wheels go round " is the secret root of all man's science and philosophy. On these two instincts is based the School.

We have considered these instincts in pairs, and have pointed out the intimate connection of each pair with a fundamental human institution. This is a convenient way of indicating their significance. But we must remember that these instincts are rarely found in isolation, and that all of them contribute in some measure to every human institution. In the State and in the Church, in the Home and in the School, we find the same human behaviour, based on the same instincts and governed by the same laws. All our experience is a unity. But within this unity some modes of instinctive behaviour are more closely connected than others with one or other of the chief human institutions.

§ 4. **The Education of Instinct.** All that has been said in the previous sections implies that instincts can be educated. The possibility of educating them depends on their three chief characteristics. (1) Instincts are inherited. They are there to start with, and thus are material ready to the hand of the educator. (2) Instincts are modifiable. Within their limits they may be wonderfully developed by training. (3) Instincts are general. The specific activities which result from them may largely be determined by education.

All instincts are valuable when they are of "just right" strength. But when they become unduly weak or excessively violent, they may be injurious both to the individual himself and to the community of which he is a member. This is true of all the instincts. (1) The instinct of shrinking is socially valuable, when it is of the "just right" degree of strength. There are some things from which we are naturally averse, which we instinctively shun. It is right that we should shrink from them. But if the instinct of shrinking be too strong, it is apt to produce cowardice. On the other hand, if it be too weak, it may lead to insensibility and hardness of nature. And if we extend the moral significance of the instinct, it becomes even more clear that either in excess or in deficiency it is socially injurious. It is right that a man should feel aversion to moral evil, but if the instinct be too strong, it may impel him simply to avoid contact with a social wrong, though it may be his duty to face it and try to overcome it. On the other hand, if the instinct be unduly weak, it may produce an immorally complaisant attitude to evil. (2) The proper degree of pugnacity is socially valuable. But if the instinct be unduly developed, it leads to the evils of quarrelsomeness and war. On the other hand, a deficiency in this instinct is apt to make a child a milksop. Obstacles in his path will never call out the impulse to overcome them. He will tend to be intellectually weak and morally smug. (3) The immense value of curiosity in the development of science and religion has already been mentioned. But an abnormal degree of curiosity, or curiosity developed in a wrong direction, is simply inquisitiveness, which is a social nuisance. And a child devoid of all curiosity is apt to remain a cipher. He will have no interest in what he is made to learn, and throughout his life he will be content to take the line of least resistance. (4) The "just right" degree of the complementary instincts of self-assertiveness and self-abasement is socially valuable. At their "just right" degree these instincts become identical in their operation. Instinctive behaviour which shows the "just right" amount of self-assertiveness will also exhibit the "just right" degree of self-abasement. But we all know that excessive self-assertion is socially injurious, and so is excessive self-abasement. (5) The value of the gregarious instinct in its proper degree has already been referred to. Where it is lacking a man is apt to become a recluse and even a misanthrope. On the other hand, where it is unduly strong, it produces a pernicious love of the crowd. We see the operation of this instinct in an aggravated form (and compounded, no doubt, with other influences) in the herding of people into cities, in the love of perambulating busy streets, in attendance at crowded picture-palaces and football matches. (6) The instinct of acquisitiveness, in its proper degree, is the secret of provision for the future and of all social progress. Where it is absent or deficient, we have the vices of improvidence and prodigality. When it appears in excessive strength, it gives rise to miserliness and hoarding for its own sake. Both in excess and defect it is socially injurious. (7) The sexual instinct is socially valuable only in its right degree. Excessive strength and undue weakness will equally lead to disastrous social results. (8) The same is true of the parental instinct.

Thus in the case of every instinct the "just right" degree is personally valuable and socially useful; while excess or defect in the strength of the instinct is disadvantageous.

It is the task of the moral educator to secure that these instincts shall be developed to the "just right" degree, and in the right directions. If one child is always eager to "punch" his neighbour, his excessive pugnacity must be restrained. If another is perpetually bored, his curiosity should be stimulated. If another suffers from excessive shyness, his self-assertiveness should be encouraged. In each case it should be the aim of the teacher to confirm the instinct in its "just right" degree.

But a great difficulty arises here. What is the "just right" degree? The teacher may know quite well what is the "just right" degree of the instincts he possesses. He knows that they are "just right" precisely as he knows that the temperature of his bath is "just right." He does not require a thermometer, when he is healthy, to tell him when his bath is "just right"; and when he is morally healthy, he needs no moral thermometer to tell him that his instincts are "just right."[1]

But the teacher must beware of thinking that what is "just right" for him is necessarily "just right" for all his pupils. In one of his plays Judge Parry brings in a machine for measuring the goodness and naughtiness of boys and girls. A boy steps on the machine, and the indicator points to "good as gold." A little girl is next tested, and the verdict is "bad as blacking." But if we could have such a machine, it would be quite useless. Character cannot be weighed or measured like height or weight, and a degree of instinct which is quite right in one child may be quite wrong in another. Much therefore depends on the discretion and experience of the teacher. The teacher must learn by experience what is the "just right" degree of an instinct in a particular child. The mother learns by feeling the water what is the "just right" temperature of the baby's bath; and if she has twins, she may find by experience that the "just right" temperature for one is not "just right" for the other. The teacher must use his discretion in judging what is the "just right" degree of any instinct in a particular pupil; and must be ready to permit his experience of the child to modify his judgment. In particular, the teacher must always be prepared to allow for individual idiosyncrasies, and beware of reducing all his pupils to a dull mediocrity. He should remember that at the best he is an adviser, whose task is to encourage the child and co-operate with him.

[1] Cf. Burnet: *Aristotle on Education*, p. 66.

§ 5. Instinctive Behaviour and Moral Conduct.

The simpler instincts tend to secure, at least at first, merely the physical safety of the individual to whom they belong. The animal's instincts are all directed to self-preservation. At a very early date the chick's instincts render it capable of taking care of itself. Its instincts end, as they began, in the tendency to self-preservation and the preservation of the race. The child's instincts are not so entirely self-preservative : they do not need to be so wholly directed to self-preservation. Its parents look after it for a relatively long period. Thus the child's instincts may be developed and moralised and extended to contribute to more comprehensive ends. They tend not merely to self-preservation, but to the realisation of all the capacities of the child, mental and moral as well as physical. As the child rises above the merely instinctive level, and develops conscious purposes, he comes to will his actions, and his behaviour becomes *conduct*. Instead of instinctively acting merely with a view to self-preservation, he forms definite purposes, directed to the complete realisation of his powers. His instinctive modes of behaviour are organised and developed to contribute to the comprehensive ends which he sets before himself as those which it is his duty to achieve in fulfilling his vocation. All that this gradual process of moralisation and organisation involves will be explained in subsequent chapters.

For further reading : G. F. Stout : *Manual of Psychology*, bk. iii. pt. i. ch. i. ; W. M'Dougall : *Social Psychology*, ch. ii., iii., x.-xiv. ; C. Lloyd Morgan : *Instinct and Experience*, ch. i.-iv.

CHAPTER IV.

IMPULSE AND DESIRE.

§ 1. **Impulse and Instinct.** We have seen that instincts lead to certain types of action. The pugnacious instinct, for example, is responsible for the readiness of the normal boy to fight on the slightest provocation, or on none at all. The instinct of pugnacity gives rise to the impulse to strike. Again, the instinct of curiosity immediately prompts the child to explore with its hands the object that excites its interest. Or the instinct will drive the child to investigate the fire, until a sharp lesson teaches it that some impulses must be restrained. In every case impulse is intimately connected with instinct. Impulsive behaviour may be defined as instinct in action. An impulse is the executive aspect of an instinct.

The actions of the young child are almost all impulsive. They are done on the spur of the moment. Offer two apples of different sizes to a young child, and he will at once take the larger one.[1] The impulse simply exerts itself without

[1] It is instructive, as an instance of the way in which moral education is apt to defeat itself, to notice what may happen when the child has been taught that its impulse to grab the

let or hindrance. The frank impulsiveness of the child is often very attractive. But impulsive behaviour which would be charming in the child might be detestable in the adult. We say that the adult ought to be able to control his impulses.

Impulses are isolated. There is no continuity between one impulsive action and another. Impulsive behaviour is stimulated simply by the needs and interests of the moment. Hence there is nothing stable or constant about impulsive behaviour. The uncertainty and capriciousness of impulses become very evident when they conflict. For example, a young child is set on the floor on the other side of the room from its mother and father, who are sitting on either side of the fire. For fun the father tries to attract the child to come to him, and the mother seeks to entice it to come to her. The child is obviously swayed, as we can see by its "wobbling," now by the impulse to go to its mother, now by that to go to its father. The impulses immediately impel it in one direction or the other, and it simply obeys the impulse which is strongest at the moment.

§ 2. **The Control of Impulse.** As the child's character develops, it gradually comes to control its impulses. It reflects, in a rudimentary way, on the alternatives when two impulses affect it, and it deliberates whether to obey the one or the

---

larger apple is selfish and naughty. It is taught (*a*) that it is wrong to grab—"let others have their choice before you," and (*b*) that it is wrong to take the biggest. Now the child is very apt, next time apples are offered to it, to pass them to others before helping itself, because it knows that they will take the smaller ones, and thus the big one will be left for it.

IMPULSE AND DESIRE

other. Thus its conduct becomes consistent, instead of being at the mercy of everything it happens to see and every thought or mental image that occurs to it. The possibility of rational conduct depends on the control of impulse. The child has been burnt when it has gone too near the fire, in obedience to its impulse to satisfy its curiosity. Later on, the same impulse to investigate the gleaming, glowing thing will recur. The child may be swayed by this impulse again, but it will also be moved by the impulse to avoid the thing that has previously given it pain. It may repress the former impulse simply because its dread of being burnt is stronger than its curiosity. In this case one impulse has overcome the other. But the child cannot be said to control its impulses until it knows what the fire is, and why it should not approach too close to it. If it knows this, it is able to reflect, in a rudimentary way, and to dismiss the impulse to explore the fire, not because it has been over-mastered by a stronger impulse, but because it has been controlled by reason.

Thus one of the conditions of controlling impulse is knowledge. The animals are at the mercy of their impulses because they have no knowledge. But man can "look before and after"; he can deliberate on his impulses and reflect whether the actions to which they impel will be valuable to his life as a whole. Thus even the every-day knowledge that the child is acquiring in school and elsewhere is fitting him more and more to reflect on his impulses and thus to restrain those that tend to unworthy ends.

But it is a matter of common experience that it is not enough merely to know that an impulse is unworthy. We may know that it is wrong, and still allow it to translate itself into action. We may, indeed, feel powerless to stop it. Take, for instance, this striking case. "A nurse, a gentle, peaceable creature as a rule, during her mistress's absence one day felt an irresistible impulse to cut the throat of the little child she was nursing, with a knife that she saw on the table, and this though she was devoted to the child. She ran into the kitchen with the knife, threw it away, and begged the cook to keep near her. The cook refused. The irresistible inclination to murder the child came on again, and she would probably have done it, had not her mistress returned in the nick of time. Later on she admitted what awful torture these impulses had been to her." [1] But we do not need to go to such extreme and abnormal cases for examples of the overpowering strength of impulses. Most of us can think of occasions in our own experience when we have acted on impulse, though we were perfectly well aware of the unworthiness of the impulse. When we thus allow an impulse to become an action in contravention of our better judgment, it shows that our lives are not yet completely under the dominion of our wills. The open secret of controlling our impulses lies in "putting them in their proper place," in bringing them into subjection to the self as a whole, which, as conscience, is able to judge them, and, as will, is able either to restrain them or bring them into action.

[1] Störring : *Mental Pathology*, p. 286.

IMPULSE AND DESIRE

§ 3. Desire. Desires may be regarded, at least from one standpoint, as developed impulses. As *developed* impulses, they differ in two respects from mere impulses. (*a*) When we act on impulse, the end that we aim at is not usually clearly present to us. In purely impulsive behaviour we are impelled in a certain direction without clearly knowing why. On the other hand, when we desire, we know the end we wish to attain, and we definitely desire *something*. (*b*) As we have seen, impulses are isolated and temporary. If an impulse be restrained, it disappears. Impulses do not persist long at the same time, though they may recur again and again. But desires are relatively permanent. If an end that is desired is comprehensive enough, the desire for it may last a life-time. Of course, desires vary in their permanence. Many of our desires are quite capricious. But, on the whole, desires are more permanent and consistent than impulses.

Desires, like impulses, may conflict. Usually a desire for a comprehensive end is opposed by a transient and isolated desire. A student may desire to pass a certain examination. If the examination be a long way ahead, *e.g.* a Civil Service Examination, the desire to pass it will organise all his studies for years previously. And it will often happen that other desires will conflict with the comprehensive desire to pass the examination. Six months before his examination, he is offered a trip to America. He greatly desires to go, but he knows that it will interfere with his preparation for his examination. If he deliberates well, he will decide for the more comprehensive desire. But he is very apt to be enticed by the more immediate satisfaction which the trip to America offers.

§ 4. **The Education of Desire.** In order that the moral life may be harmonious, desires must be educated and trained.

(1) Desires should be selected. It is a great mistake to think that *all* desires should be restrained. Sometimes we are told that morality consists in suppressing our desires and being content to see the world that it is good. The Stoics tell us that we should acquiesce, with passive contentment, in any lot which fortune has seen fit to assign to us. Desires, they say, are mischievous, and they should be destroyed. But this is quite wrong. Every child has a myriad desires. They cannot *all* be satisfied, and it is not well that they should be. But these desires should not be suppressed wholesale. To suppress all desires is to close the safety-valve of character. Sooner or later, if healthy desires are repressed, a moral eruption will result.

Again, we sometimes speak of controlling desires as if, like Plato, we pictured them as unruly horses which need to be reined in. Impulses may have to be controlled in this way; but desires are not so isolated as impulses, and we control desires most effectively not by holding in those which are evil, but by strengthening those that are socially valuable and giving rein to them.

If the child's desires are good, then they should by all means be confirmed and encouraged. There is a natural selection among desires, but if the desires are left to themselves, the fittest will not always survive. The moral educator must throw all his weight on the side of the good desires. If they are strengthened and confirmed, the evil ones will gradually be ousted and overcome.

(2) The child should be encouraged to organise his desires. It is here especially that the teacher may expect to be able to exercise a real influence. He can point out that certain desires are inconsistent with other more comprehensive desires, and therefore should not be satisfied. As we grow older we naturally and unconsciously organise our desires. The character of saint or sinner depends on the fact that their desires have been organised in subordination to some comprehensive good or bad end. The infant's desires are at first little more than impulses, and they are aroused by everything he hears and sees. They are comparatively isolated, and their objects are desired for themselves and not with a view to any more comprehensive end. The infant desires the coin the visitor shows him, simply because it looks an interesting thing, and not for the sake of anything it can buy. As the child grows up, his desires become less capricious. He comes to have some idea why he desires things. But still things are desired largely on their own account. The child does not take large views, and rarely has comprehensive aims. Yet, even when his aims are very limited, his desires naturally become organised with reference to them. Take the case of education. The young child desires to know his lesson, in order to " get top " of the class. This is certainly a very limited end, and in the young child it may be the only end of his desire.

But he soon grows to desire to "get top" in order to satisfy the more comprehensive end of getting a prize. It is often remarkable how such a relatively restricted aim as this may organise the child's desires and activities. He will himself curb his desire for play in order to prepare his home lessons. His desire for a perfect school attendance will enable him to overcome a violent desire to accept his uncle's invitation to a pantomime some afternoon. In these ways he is organising his desires with reference to some relatively permanent and comprehensive aim. The great purpose of moral education is to encourage the organisation of desires under some worthy end. Right desires are as important for the child as true knowledge. It has been said, and with much truth, that the great aim of all education is to teach men and women to desire the right things.

So far we have been following common usage in speaking of "good desires" and "evil desires." But these phrases conceal an important distinction, which must now be explained. When we speak of "good desires," we are apt to confuse two meanings of the word desire. Desire properly means the actual process of desiring. But it is often used to mean the thing desired, the object of desire. When we say that a man's desires are evil, we do not mean that his actual mental processes are evil, but that the objects to whose attainment those processes are directed are, in relation to himself, evil. Desire is always for some object, and it is the goodness or badness of that object in relation to the self that makes the desire good or evil. In strictness, we

IMPULSE AND DESIRE

should not speak of desires (in the plural) at all. There is *one* process of desiring, a process which may be directed to the attainment of this or that kind of object.

Now, if this be so, are we able to explain why people desire such very different kinds of objects? Or to relapse into the more usual language, why do people have such very different desires? At the present moment you may desire a knowledge of Italian, I a pork pie. Why do I desire the pork pie, and why do you desire a knowledge of Italian? The answer is that objects are always desired in reference to the self. They become objects of desire only because they have some value for the self that desires them. Hence what has value for one man may have none for another. Men desire only those objects on which they set some value, and they set a value on them because they promise a satisfaction of the self. Incidentally we may note that the reason why all men desire money is that money is potentially all that money can buy. Money is a standard of value because money can be turned into many of the objects which men desire. Money is not desired for itself, but because it can buy the objects in which the most different kinds of people find satisfaction.

All the objects of desire, whether purchasable by money or not, owe their moral worth to their relation to some self. *In themselves*, these objects of desire, or the sums of money that buy them, are neither good nor bad. Their moral goodness or badness springs from their relation to the self, and their connection with its dominant purposes and aims.

§ 5. **Ambition, the System of Desire.** When a man's desires are organised in subordination to his self, with the system of its purposes, they constitute his ambition. A man's ambition is simply the system of his desires and purposes. Nothing organises a life so effectively and worthily as a noble ambition. If we wish for an example of the systematising power of a great ambition, we need only look at the way in which all St. Paul's activities and desires were organised in accordance with his noble ambition. A worthy ambition is within the reach of all. Every child should be encouraged to form a worthy ambition: every one should be reminded that there is some position in life, however humble, which he will fill, and that his vocation consists in performing faithfully the duties of his station in society. It should be his ambition to organise all his desires and consecrate all his energies to the service of his vocation.

For further reading: T. Loveday and J. A. Green: *Introduction to Psychology*, ch. vi.; J. S. Mackenzie: *Manual of Ethics*, bk. i. ch. i.; A. F. Shand: *Foundations of Character*, bk. iii.; T. H. Green: *Prolegomena to Ethics*, §§ 118-129.

CHAPTER V.

EMOTION AND SENTIMENT.

IN the last chapter we saw that impulses and desires are developed from the instinctive level of human behaviour, and enter into man's comprehensive aims, purposes, and ambitions. In the present chapter we shall consider, as a parallel evolution, the growth of man's emotions, which, instinctive in their origin, become developed and systematised into comprehensive sentiments which may govern his whole life. Emotions and sentiments are important elements in character for many reasons, but particularly because they bear with them an immediate sense of worth or value. They impart a glow and tone to existence, and without them character would be dull and cold and hard. It is of the utmost importance that the emotions and sentiments of the child should be developed in the right way and in the right direction. We must therefore ask, What are emotions and sentiments, and how, if at all, may they be educated ?

§ 1. **The General Characteristics of Emotion.** In the text-books we find long lists of particular emotions—fear, anger, hope, suspense, jealousy, disgust, and so on. When these emotions are described, it is easy for us to recognise them and admit that they are separate emotions. But our difficulty is that when we actually experience emotions, they often seem hopelessly confused and jumbled. Take, for example, the emotional condition of a small boy who is being caned, or that of a girl who is saying good-bye to her brother " off to the Front." The small boy is probably not aware of his emotions as emotions ; and while the girl will recognise her state as an emotional one, she will make no effort to distinguish one emotion from another within that complex state. But, of course, that does not mean that the complex emotional state cannot be analysed. This is obvious if we compare our sensations in looking at a complex colour-scheme. Take, for example, our colour-sensations during the final scene of a gorgeously-dressed pantomime. The variously-coloured dresses and scenery, with all their subtle and delicate shades and tinges, blend into one complex colour-scheme. We enjoy the complex sensation we have as we observe the scene, and we do not usually try to analyse it. But, of course, the colour-scheme can be analysed. It would be quite possible to pick out all the minute shades which blend harmoniously in the whole, and quite possible also to reduce them all to the primary colours out of which they had been compounded.

Precisely the same thing is true of our complex emotional states. It is possible to analyse them. If we examine the emotional state of the boy who is being caned, we may find the emotion of anger (at himself for getting into the scrape, at the master

EMOTION AND SENTIMENT

who told "the Head" about it, and at "the Head" himself for inflicting the pain); the emotion of suspense, as he watches the descending cane; perhaps the emotion of fear of the pain it will cause; the emotion of jealousy of the boy who was in the same scrape and was not caught; and, it may be, disgust with himself for "blubbing." Again, if we analyse the emotions of the girl who is saying good-bye to her soldier-brother, we may find that her emotional state includes fear lest her brother be killed; anger at the Germans for causing the war; the suspense of wishing now that the train would go, now that it would give a little longer time to say good-bye; hope that he will be kept safe; jealousy of his fiancée, who is occupying too much of his attention, and so on.

These states are very complex. But, as we have seen, they can be analysed into a number of simple or primary emotions. These primary emotions often occur alone. The child who is struck by another immediately feels the emotion of anger, the creak of the door in the small hours immediately excites the emotion of fear, and so on.

Let us now consider some of the general characteristics of emotion. (1) Emotions permeate the whole of life. They impart glow and colour and tone to existence. Very little of our normal waking life is altogether devoid of emotion. But people differ very greatly in their susceptibility to emotion. Many a dull, drab life seems to have lost altogether any capacity it ever had to be emotionally affected. Emotion is a specially "human" characteristic, and we often call a man who has no capacity for emotion, or never allows himself to be moved by emotion, "inhuman."

(2) Emotions are for the most part instinctive in their origin. The child does not need to learn to feel angry or afraid. The simpler and coarser emotions, such as anger, fear, and jealousy, are more completely instinctive than the finer and more complex ones.

(3) Emotions are generally excited by some specific stimulus or some definite situation. In the latter respect they resemble impulses, which usually arise in response to some special need or interest. Some stimulus, *e.g.* a blow or an insult, is necessary to excite the emotion of anger. And some definite situation, *e.g.* a concert or a parting, is needed to produce complex emotional states. Emotions may also be excited by the recollection of some definite situation. The emotional state of the convert at the revival meeting is often produced more by his recollection of his good mother and his wasted life than by the preacher's actual words.

(4) The emotion may persist long after the stimulus has disappeared. If one has been angered early in the morning, the emotion may continue all day in a dull subconscious sort of way. If one has wakened up at night with the fear that burglars are in the house, it may take a long time for the emotion to disappear entirely. But perhaps the most persistent and constant of human emotions is hope. "Hope springs eternal in the human breast."

Such an emotion which persists after the situation in which it originated has passed may be called an emotional disposition. An emotional disposition is more indefinite than a simple emotion. A simple emotion always has a reference to some definite object. We are afraid of some thing or some person, we are angry at some thing or some person. But an emotional disposition is vague and general. It is a tendency to be easily excited to a certain emotion. Thus an emotional disposition of irritability, resulting from a definite fit of anger, will make us, while it lasts, more susceptible to anger than we are normally.

(5) The objects or situations which excite emotions in one person may have no effect on others. Emotions are relative to persons just as desires are. What is an object of desire to me may leave you quite cold. Similarly, what excites my emotions may have no effect whatever on you. The Englishman feels disgust at eating frogs, and the German feels disgust at the thought of eating rabbits. Many a man experiences a violent emotion of fear on seeing a black cat. One man's emotions may be affected by Handel's *Largo*, another's by *Alexander's Ragtime Band*. The teacher should bear in mind that it is not to be expected that the same emotion will be evoked in every child by the same situation.

(6) Emotions naturally express themselves in our physical appearance or behaviour. This fact has been vigorously stated by William James. "What kind of an emotion of fear would be left if the feeling neither of quickened heart-beats nor of shallow breathing, neither of trembling lips nor of weakened limbs, neither of gooseflesh nor of visceral stirrings, were present, it is quite impossible for me to think. Can one fancy the state of rage, and picture no ebullition in the chest, no flushing of the face, no

dilatation of the nostrils, no clenching of the teeth, no impulse to vigorous action, but in their stead limp muscles, calm breathing, and a placid face ? "[1] But it is not only intense emotions that give rise to organic sensations and physical expressions. Organic changes, *e.g.* alteration in the rate of pulse-beat or breathing, accompany a slight touch of irritation just as they do a wild fit of rage.

§ 2. **The Control and Organisation of Emotion.** Children and savages naturally allow full scope to their emotions. Their emotions are readily excited, and they do nothing to control their expressions. In the child or the savage the emotion of anger immediately gives rise to the impulse to strike, and the impulse is generally obeyed. One of the first lessons the child has to learn is the necessity of restraining its emotions. It has to be made to realise that there are other persons in the world besides itself, and that its actions have been probably such as would naturally arouse angry feelings in the other person also. But the other person has learned to control that emotion.

Emotions may best be kept under restraint by controlling their expressions. The child soon learns to control the movements of his limbs. When he is angry he must not kick or strike. Again, he must restrain the vocal expression of his emotions, or at least of some of them. He must not scream when he is angry. He takes longer to learn to control the facial expression of emotion. And it is not desirable that we should have our emotions so completely under control that they never display themselves in

[1] *Principles of Psychology*, ii. p. 452.

our features. In general, we strive to conceal only those emotions of which we are ashamed. We seek to overcome blushing, because it "gives us away." We strive to prevent our faces paling with fear, because that is an emotion of which we are ashamed. Many of our emotions we have so far under control that we allow them to express themselves on some occasions, but not on others. We would allow the emotion of anger to express itself on our faces and in our words and actions, if we thought the occasion demanded righteous indignation. On the other hand, a similarly violent emotion might be repressed, if we thought its expression wrong or inexpedient. And there are other emotions whose expression on the face few people can wholly prevent.

Three things have specially to be remembered in connection with the control of emotion.

(1) There is no virtue in restraining the expression of our emotions unless we are thus helped to control the emotions themselves. The great practical importance of controlling the expression of emotion lies in the fact that if it is regularly and strictly controlled, the emotion itself is less apt to be evoked on future occasions by the appropriate stimulus. The importance of controlling the expression consists in the added ability it gives us to control the emotion itself. "And it seems probable that in societies such as our own, where control over the expression of emotion is inculcated from an early age, emotions are, as a rule, actually less intense than among peoples who see no cause for shame in giving them comparatively free play."[1]

[1] Loveday and Green: *Psychology*, p. 138.

It would be a very dull and uninteresting world, if we all controlled the facial expression of our emotions. Conversation and social intercourse would lose half their charm, if the social emotions were not expressed on our faces. The difference between a vivacious and a dull person often depends largely on the expressiveness of their features. And a more distinctively ethical question is involved. The habitual concealment of our emotions is apt to encourage a general tendency to dissimulation.

Further, it is not desirable that all emotions should be suppressed. To subdue all emotions is to rob life of much of its glow and warmth. It is as disastrous to deprive life of its emotions as it is to destroy all its desires. But not every form of emotion is valuable either to the individual or to the society of which he is a member. The emotions of jealousy and fear, for instance, are not in general desirable. But the energy that expresses itself in these emotions may be diverted into socially valuable directions. The energy that would express itself in jealousy may be turned into emulation, and fear may be transmuted into the emotion of respect. The moral educator may become the Alchymist of Character.

(2) Emotions should be allowed to work themselves out in activity of some kind. Nothing is worse than simply to bottle up emotions. Pent-up emotions "work like madness in the brain." If the emotion is simply dammed up it may breed poison in the moral life of the child, or it may later strike out a socially injurious path for itself. If anger be simply pent-up, it may become a brooding spirit of revenge, which may emerge later on in an activity of a far

EMOTION AND SENTIMENT

more harmful kind. The ill effects of pent-up grief are well known, and a flood of tears may bring wonderful relief.

In many cases the emotional energy may be directed into other and more valuable channels. It may be transmuted into cognitive or conative energy. " To a certain extent, whatever currents are diverted from the regions below must swell the activity of the thought-tracts of the brain."[1] The emotional power that has been excited should not be allowed simply to accumulate as a dead weight. Nor should it be permitted to evaporate without bearing some practical fruit. "There is no more contemptible type of character than that of the nerveless sentimentalist and dreamer, who spends his life in a weltering sea of sensibility and emotion, but who never does a manly concrete deed. Rousseau, inflaming all the mothers of France, by his eloquence, to follow Nature and nurse their babies themselves, while he sends his own children to the foundling hospital, is the classical example of what I mean. The habit of excessive novel-reading and theatre-going will produce true monsters in this line. The weeping of a Russian lady over the fictitious personages in the play, while her coachman is freezing to death on the seat outside, is the sort of thing that everywhere happens on a less glaring scale. . . . The remedy would be never to suffer oneself to have an emotion at a concert without expressing it afterwards in *some* active way. Let the expression be the least thing in the world—speaking genially to one's aunt, or giving up one's seat in a horse-car,

[1] James: *Principles of Psychology,* ii. p. 466.

if nothing more heroic offers—but let it not fail to take place." [1] It is one of the great tasks of moral education to secure that emotions issue in valuable channels. Children should be encouraged to seek for themselves worthy outlets for their emotions. It is a wise moral economy to translate emotion into socially valuable action.

(3) Emotions are most valuable when they appear in an organised life. In every department of mental and moral activity aimlessness is both unpleasant and unprofitable. The child is never emotionally satisfied unless it is occupied in some way. The very young child's life is organised round such primary needs as eating and playing and sleeping. It wants toys to keep it amused, and when the old toys' possibilities become exhausted, the child's life becomes disorganised. It frets and fumes, and the emotions of jealousy and fear are developed. In the school, also, it is essential that the child should be kept fully occupied. Otherwise it becomes listless, and its emotional state, which was previously kept at a more or less high level of pleasurable activity, sinks to the depths of boredom and irritability. The unpleasantness of waiting for a train that is late is due to the absence of aim and occupation. We have time which we cannot organise in any way: the moments must simply be allowed to slip away in dull suspense. In order to escape the unpleasant emotional condition of boredom, we must organise our mental activities. And as we are most often bored during leisure hours, it follows that it is one of the great tasks of education to train children in the right

[1] James : *Op. cit.* i. pp. 125-126.

enjoyment of leisure. Only so will the emotional disposition be maintained at a high level.

The emotions themselves must be organised. The educationist's aim is not to encourage each and every emotion. Emotions good and valuable in themselves may become positively mischievous if they are allowed to riot at haphazard. There is no more futile life than the existence that is at the mercy of random emotions. And it is important to notice that such an unsystematic condition is not natural. "Mental activity tends, at first unconsciously, afterwards consciously, to produce and to sustain system and organisation."[1] The possibility of organising the emotions depends on the fact that they are always excited by, or cluster round, perceptions or ideas which are to a certain extent in our own power. The emotion of jealousy may be roused equally by the sight of my rival or by the thought of him. A great many of our emotions are excited by imagination or recollection rather than by actual perception or sensation. This is an important point in connection with their organisation. For our trains of thoughts and images are more under our control than our perceptions. We cannot always choose what we shall perceive; but it is always possible for us to determine what thoughts and images should live in our experience. We can organise them in accordance with our dominant purposes and ideals. And in this way we can organise the emotions which are connected with them.

§ 3. **Sentiments.** Emotions may be organised into sentiments. In the young child emotions occur as

[1] Shand: *The Foundations of Character*, p. 21.

disconnectedly as impulses. In the last chapter we saw that impulses gradually become organised into more or less fixed desires. Similarly, the isolated emotions of the child become organised into more or less permanent attitudes, which we call sentiments. The emotions of the young child come and go quickly, one moment tears, the next smiles. But sentiments do not change in this way. They are gradually produced, and it is only gradually that they can be modified. One of the first sentiments that the child develops is love for his parents. When we say that the child loves his parents, we do not mean merely that he has from moment to moment a certain affectionate emotion towards them, but that he has a more or less fixed disposition or attitude to them, which may include many special emotions, *e.g.* sorrow when they are angry with him, jealousy of his little brother who is being petted, or joy when their affection seems to be restored to him.

Sentiments arise most naturally in connection with persons, and they have an intimate relation to character. The child enters into relations with his parents, relatives, teachers, and other friends; and out of these relations grow his sentiments. Sentiments are nearly all varieties of love or hatred, of like or dislike. If the child develops sentiments towards things, it is because he really regards them as persons. The little girl treats her doll and her teddy-bear as persons, and her sentiment towards them dies away precisely when it becomes too great an effort of imagination to credit them with personal behaviour. As the child grows up, he extends the sentiment of love which originated in his attitude to his parents to groups of persons and institutions. He develops a love of his school, of his city, of his country, and of his religion. In every case the sentiment is fundamentally love, though it may be called loyalty, patriotism, or enthusiasm.

When sentiments conflict, it may be either with other sentiments or with emotions. The child's love of his parents may conflict with his momentary anger at them. The sentiment of avarice may conflict with patriotism or filial love. When two sentiments conflict, that one will conquer which has been most habitually at one with the character as a whole. In every conflict between sentiment and emotion, the sentiment is likely to overcome the emotion which opposes it. The emotion owes its strength to its suddenness and intensity; but it soon exhausts itself, and the sentiment with which it clashed remains dominant. It is a sign of moral progress when the sentiment completely controls and organises the emotions and desires of life in accordance with its own end. It is a fundamental moral law, according to Mr. Shand, that " in the growth of character, the sentiments tend, with increasing success, to control the emotions and impulses ; in the decline of character, the emotions and impulses tend, with increasing power, to achieve their freedom." [1]

There is a certain stability about sentiments. They are not swayed by every gust of feeling. They are gradually formed, and though they may be subsequently modified, this will not be done easily or quickly. There is something morally conservative about sentiments. Our sentiments often persist

[1] *Op. cit.* p. 62.

even when both reason and feeling in us brand them as unworthy. There are Germans to-day who *know* that Germany did wrong to hack its way through Belgium, and *feel* a righteous indignation with her for doing it ; and yet their patriotism and loyalty to their fatherland is as strong as ever. Sentiments, once formed, are profoundly conservative forces.

Sentiments vary very much from one man to another. They differ much more than emotions do. In the same community the most diverse sentiments may be found. In one man the sentiment of the family may be the strongest thing in the world, in another the sentiment of patriotism, or loyalty to some institution, or enthusasm for the kingdom of God, while others may be dominated by the selfish sentiment, the sentiment of self-love. Now sentiments are almost wholly acquired during the lifetime of the man in whom they appear. The hereditary element in them is very slight. Sentiments are developed under the influence of the social environment.

Hence the importance of the moral education of the sentiments. The sentiments are essentially educable, and their formed nature depends wholly on how the child has been trained. Whether the child will become a patriotic citizen or a neutral cipher, a loyal member of a family or a self-centred misanthrope, an enthusiast for social righteousness or a morbid egoist, will depend very largely on the influence of parents and teachers.

What practical steps can the teacher take in attempting to educate the sentiments ? It is not advisable simply to describe such a sentiment as

EMOTION AND SENTIMENT

patriotism and inculcate it, with much exhortation, as a virtue. That is often the very worst way to instil a sentiment. For a sentiment is a kind of feeling ; and a feeling can never be made to seem desirable simply by being described. The only way to encourage the growth of sentiments is to make the great ends with which they are connected seem desirable as the great aims of life. In practice, the teaching of History may be used to foster the sentiments of patriotism and loyalty, just as the teaching of Scripture ought to aim at the stimulation of an enthusiasm for humanity.

The moral importance of the sentiments cannot be gainsaid. Every sentiment encourages the growth of those qualities of character which seem likely to subserve its ends. Patriotism or religious zeal stimulate special sets of virtues ; and, in general, we may say with Mr. Shand, that " every sentiment tends to acquire the virtues and vices that are required by its system." [1] Love, for instance, fosters a whole galaxy of good qualities ; but it is apt also to acquire the defects of its virtues, such as jealousy and partiality. Love must ever be partial, and hence may often be unjust.

A profound sentiment will pervade the whole of a man's life, constantly spurring him on to fresh efforts. A great love, whether for a person or for a cause or institution, influences the man in whom it burns to strain every nerve to make himself more worthy of the service of the beloved person or cause. He feels it necessary to harmonise his life as a whole in accordance with the purposes of his dominant

[1] *Op. cit.* p. 110.

sentiment. All the strength of his will is directed to support the sentiment. The more intensely and steadfastly a man loves a person or institution, the more completely he organises his whole life round this sentiment.

For further reading : A. F. Shand : *The Foundations of Character* ; W. James : *Principles of Psychology*, ii. ch. xxv. ; W. M'Dougall : *Social Psychology*, ch. v.-vii.; H. H. Horne : *Psychological Principles of Education*, part iii.

CHAPTER VI.

THE MORAL SELF.

§ 1. **The Growth of the Self.** In former chapters, in dealing with the child's instincts, his impulses and desires, and his emotions and sentiments, we have seen that all involve some reference to the self. But we have not yet asked, What is the self? That question we must now try to answer. It will be convenient to begin by describing how the child first comes to recognise the existence of his self.

At first, of course, the child has no distinct notion of its "self." It gradually comes to realise that its body belongs to it in a peculiar way. It plays with its fingers and toes, and finds that it has more control over them than the fingers of its mother, with which it also plays. It becomes conscious, too, that it has *feeling* in its fingers and toes. These things belong specially to it; and thus the self comes to mean the body. But gradually this conception of self becomes both extended and narrowed.

On the one hand, the conception of the self is widened. The child comes to regard the persons to whom it is related and the things which come into its possession as part of itself. Its mother and father have a peculiarly intimate relation to it, and they come to be regarded as part of the self. Clothes, too, become part of the self. Even in the case of the very young child, clothing seems peculiarly personal. The child feels abased if its clothing is not to its taste. Again, it feels personally elevated when it is attired in a new dress. The self also comes to include other possessions. Toys and dolls, balls and coins, all these form part of the self, and the child feels deprived of part of itself when the favourite doll or toy cannot be found. As the child grows up, those portions of his property which he has himself made seem more closely identified with himself than others. If these be lost, he experiences a shrinkage of personality. He feels literally smaller. The home also becomes identified with himself. If he leaves for good the home in which all his early experiences have been gained, he feels as if he had really abandoned part of his real self. Hence the self comes to mean all that the man is or has. " In its widest possible sense, a man's self is the sum total of all that he *can* call his, not only his body and his psychic powers, but his clothes and his house, his wife and his children, his ancestors and his friends, his reputation and works, his lands and horses, and yacht and bank-account. All these things give him the same emotions. If they wax and prosper, he feels triumphant ; if they dwindle and die away, he feels cast down." [1]

On the other hand, the conception of the self becomes narrowed and more distinctly defined. The child realises that all he possesses is not equally himself. There is an inner core, which would remain though all his possessions should be lost and his body

[1] James : *Principles of Psychology*, i. p. 291.

THE MORAL SELF

maimed and mutilated. His self, his personality, would still exist. What exactly the pure self means is a question over which philosophers are still wrangling. We may call it, if we care, the soul or spirit or the mind or Ego; but the important point is that the self or "I" is presupposed in all we do and all we think. It is I who do this or that action; it is I who eat and sleep and think and work; it is I who have this emotion of anger, that sentiment of patriotism, this impulse to enlist, that desire to fight; it is I who am overwhelmed in a mood of despondency or am sunk in temperamental melancholy; it is I who doubt and hesitate and deliberate and reflect. All these actions and feelings and thoughts are referred to myself. They help to constitute myself; or we may say that they belong to me, that I have them. The I is the most intimate and real core of my self.

§ 2. **The Social Nature of the Self.** The child's awareness of himself develops alongside his recognition of other selves or persons. He could not become conscious of himself at all, did he not come into contact with other selves. Thus the self is thoroughly social. At first the child does not distinguish between "things" and "persons." He treats them all alike, he treats them, in fact, just as he treats himself. Tables and chairs are regarded as persons, and so are animals. But the child gradually comes to see that there are important differences between persons and things. Things are much more constant in their behaviour than persons. They can always be counted upon; they never vary. But the behaviour of persons seems to the child very capricious. Why should the nurse sometimes sing to it, and sometimes scold it ? Why does mother sometimes whip it, and sometimes kiss it ? That these variations in mother's and nurse's behaviour may be due to variations in its own behaviour does not at first occur to the child. But eventually the child recognises that it, like other persons, is a person whose behaviour is liable to change.

(a) Since persons, including itself, are apparently capricious and variable in their behaviour, they become the special objects of the child's attention. Persons are much more interesting than things. Thus the child pays special attention to its self and other selves.

(b) But the child is not content simply to attend to others. It pays attention to them in order to imitate them. The child is the most imitative of all animals. Up to the age of seven or eight, every normal child persistently imitates everything in its environment, but especially the persons with whom it comes in contact. Persons are so much easier and so much more interesting to imitate than things. The child imitates first the actions, and then the customs and habits of his parents ; and thus he may acquire many of his parents' traits. When the child resembles his parents closely in character, the similarity is usually due far more to the influence of the early home environment than to the direct inheritance of particular qualities.

The child imitates not only its parents, but also everybody with whom it comes in contact, and even the examples suggested to it by fairy tales and the ideals inspired by religious instruction. The child's personality is gradually developed, as it acquires these traits and qualities which it imitates in others. In this way it transfers to itself qualities which it sees in others, and which seem desirable to it. Prof. Baldwin has explained clearly the kind of process that takes place. " Last year I thought of my friend W. as a man who had great skill on the bicycle, and who wrote readily on the typewriter ; my sense of his personality included these accomplishments. . . . My sense of myself did not have these elements. But now, this year, I have learned to do both these things. I have taken the elements formerly recognised in W.'s personality, and by imitative learning brought them over to myself. I now think of myself as one who rides a ' wheel ' and writes on a ' machine.' . . . So the truth we now learn is this : that very many of the particular marks which I now call mine, when I think of myself, have had just this origin. I have first found them in my social environment, and by reason of my social and imitative disposition, have transferred them to myself by trying to act as if they were true of me, and so coming to find out that they are true of me." [1]

(c) But the child does not imitate *every* quality in those it sees around it. To some qualities or traits it has a natural repugnance. Its attitude to them is one of opposition. There is no doubt that many children early come to develop an attitude of opposition towards all that " grown-ups " are and do. The conduct of adults may excite opposition,

[1] *Social and Ethical Interpretations in Mental Development*, pp. 10-11.

because it is largely unintelligible. "These elders, our betters by a trick of chance, commanded no respect, but only a certain blend of envy—of their good luck—and pity—for their inability to make use of it. Indeed, it was one of the most hopeless features of their character that, having absolute licence to indulge in the pleasures of life, they could get no good of it. They might dabble in the pond all day, hunt the chickens, climb trees in the most uncompromising Sunday clothes; they were free to issue forth and buy gunpowder in the full eye of the sun—free to fire cannons and explode mines on the lawn: yet they never did any one of these things. . . . On the whole, the existence of these Olympians seemed to be entirely void of interests, even as their movements were confined and slow, and their habits stereotyped and senseless. To anything but appearances they were blind."[1] It is quite true that to many children the virtues of "grown-ups" seem flat, and their lives dull. In these cases the attitude of the child is naturally not imitative but antagonistic.

Wholesale opposition will, no doubt, be very rare, except where sympathy between parent and child is entirely absent. Where sympathy does not exist between parent and child, or between teacher and pupil, the fault is very rarely the child's. If the teacher cannot create a sympathetic atmosphere in the class-room, the children's attitude to him will be antagonistic rather than imitative. And nothing could well be more fatal to the moral education of the child.

[1] Kenneth Grahame: *The Golden Age*, pp. 4-6.

THE MORAL SELF

The facility and willingness with which the child imitates is one of the conditions of moral progress. But a slavish imitation is not desirable. It is well that the imitative attitude is usually tempered by the tendency to oppose and to originate. The child very soon learns that he ought to imitate only some qualities (those that are " good "); others it ought not to imitate (these are " bad "). Perhaps the earliest definition which the child gives to " good " is " that which ought to be imitated." It is the privilege of parents and teachers to point out what qualities ought to be imitated, and in what circumstances the child should " learn to say No."

It is important to note that from the moral standpoint these two tendencies do not need to conflict. Rather do they work together for good. The child learns that certain habits and actions should be imitated, and it follows that certain other actions and habits should be eschewed. Imitation of one set of habits leads to or implies opposition to another set.

Now, the child has not been *blindly* attending to, imitating, and opposing other persons. Everything it imitates or opposes has been contributing to the development of its own personality. The self assimilates the actions and customs which it began by imitating. They have become part of itself, closewoven into its structure. Actions which were at first performed purely imitatively, as by a parrot or monkey, and hence were not really the actions of the self, now result directly from the activity of the self. Only those actions have moral value which are the actions of a self. If a child gives a penny to a beggar, simply because it sees its mother do so, the action is not really the child's. It might equally well have been done by a monkey. But when the child really assimilates the lesson of the kind action, and gives its penny, knowing why it does so, and having a feeling of pity in its heart, then the action is really the action of the self. It is a real expression of the self or personality.

Throughout we have seen that the self is essentially social. The consciousness of self grows through intercourse with other selves. The rudimentary self of the child gains its experience and realises itself by observing and imitating and opposing the other selves in its social environment. Apart from the influence of these other selves, it would not develop at all. And the consciousness of self always includes relations to other selves. My self-consciousness contains the conviction that I am in such and such a social position. Now this social position involves a whole system of relations to other selves in the society in which I live. These relations form part of my awareness of myself. From them I weave my notion of my social position, of my duties and my rights in the community of which I am a member.

§ 3. **Personality and Vocation.** Most children, as they grow up, create in imagination the kind of self they want to be. To the oft-recurring question, "And what are you going to be ? " the child usually has a ready answer. But it may very frequently change its idea of its future self. At one time it wants to be a sailor, at another a minister. The young boy may experience great pleasure in dallying with a variety of possible selves. But the time comes when he must choose *one* of these fancied selves to be his real self.

THE MORAL SELF

One of the possible selves must be actualised. He has only one life to live, he has only one self to live it ; and if he wants to realise a character at all, he must choose some one walk in life in which to realise it.

Of course, he would *like* to be several different selves at once : all have their attractions. But he recognises that that is impossible. However severe the struggle, he must decide on some one self amid all the galaxy of his fancied selves ; and this one self must become his real self. William James has put the point very vividly. " Not that I would not, if I could, be both handsome and fat and well-dressed, and a great athlete, and make a million a year, be a wit, a *bon vivant* and a lady-killer, as well as a philosopher ; a philanthropist, statesman, warrior, and African explorer, as well as a ' tone-poet ' and saint. But the thing is simply impossible. The millionaire's work would run counter to the saint's ; the *bon vivant* and the philanthropist would trip each other up ; the philosopher and lady-killer could not well keep house in the same tenement of clay. Such different characters may conceivably at the outset of life be alike *possible* to a man. But to make any one of them actual, the rest must more or less be suppressed. So the seeker of his truest, strongest, deepest self must review the list carefully, and pick out the one on which to stake his salvation. All other selves thereupon become unreal, but the fortunes of this self are real. Its failures are real failures, its triumphs real triumphs, carrying shame and gladness with them. . . . Our thought, incessantly deciding, among many things of a kind, which ones for it shall be realities, here chooses one of many possible selves or characters." [1]

Even after it has been decided which self is to be realised, the vocation of realising this self may not be consistently followed. Many a medical student feels that his self as realised in the work of the Army or Church would be a nobler thing, many a divinity student thinks how much more useful his self would be if he had decided to actualise it in the ministry of healing the body. Somehow the *other* self which they project on the screen of their imagination seems so much finer than the one on which they have actually decided to stake their all. If they persist in dreaming about other possible selves after the possibility of realising them has passed, of course they become discontented with the walk in life which they have actually chosen. In such cases the self will never be realised as it might be. The personality will never develop to its full stature. But even when men feel that they have made a mistake in the choice of their trade or profession, they usually decide to make the best of it ; and they may come to find, with a shock of pleasant surprise, that the self may be realised in any walk of life which offers worthy work. On the whole, experience shows that for character-building it makes remarkably little difference what station in life is occupied. The farmer, the miner, the teacher, the doctor may each and all use their trades and professions as means to the development of their personality.

One reason why the particular occupation often seems to have little direct influence on the develop-

[1] *Op. cit.* i. p. 310.

ment of personality is that much of the experience which goes to the moulding of character is acquired by a man in his leisure hours. Much of it is derived from domestic and social and religious relationships, which are common to all men.

This is the explanation of the fact that the self that a man develops may not be internally consistent. A man may develop different selves, according to the different relations in which he stands to different groups of people. He may form one self in his business and another in his church. Now these selves may be discordant. The business-self may be dishonest, the religious self pious. There is an internal conflict between the two selves : the man is really trying to serve God and Mammon. But in other cases, the apparently different selves may be perfectly consistent. The officer may be stern towards the soldiers whom he commands, but as gentle as a woman towards his children. Such a self would, in reality, be perfectly harmonious, though it appears in one aspect in its attitude to one group of people, and in another aspect in relation to another group.

It is essential for a consistent moral life that the self should be harmonious. The personality must be one and constant. Its attitudes may vary in different relations and under different circumstances, but the personality as a whole should be a unity, for only then will its conduct be consistent. It is one of the great tasks of education to help the child to develop a harmonious self, to secure that his "modes of feeling, thinking, and acting show unity, consistency, and distinctive individuality." [1]

[1] *Dictionary of Philosophy and Psychology*, i. p. 173.

§ 4. **The Self and its Habits.** The importance of habit is now universally admitted, but it is not so widely recognised that habits are of no positive value until they are organised in the moral self. If our mental and moral and physical habits have been formed at haphazard, our lives will be but one stage removed from the capricious life of impulse. There is no more futile life than that which is at the mercy of chance impulses, but as a close second comes the life which is given up to habits which have grown up in accordance with no principle and in subordination to no system. A life is not morally good simply because it is composed of habits. People who have given over large tracts of their lives to habit have not always been careful to scrutinise the kinds of habits that have been formed. The full moral worth of habitual action is realised only by those who have organised their habits. Habits are organised only when they are definitely directed to serve the comprehensive ends of the self whose habits they are. The habits of the good life are systematic. They all contribute to the well-being of the self. Our habits are of our own making, and it depends on us whether they will work together for the good of the whole self. All habits are the habits of a self: they make the self, and are made by it.

The ethical importance of habit has been admirably stated by Bain and by James, and we quote four of the maxims that were enunciated by them.[1]

(1) "The great thing in education is to make our nervous system our ally instead of our enemy. . . .

---

[1] Cf. Bain: *The Emotions and the Will*, ch. ix., §§ 1-9; and James: *Principles*, vol. i., pp. 122-125.

THE MORAL SELF

For this we must make automatic and habitual, as early as possible, as many useful actions as we can, and guard against the growing into ways that are likely to be disadvantageous to us, as we should guard against the plague. The more of the details of our daily life we can hand over to the effortless custody of automatism, the more our higher powers of mind will be set free for their own proper work. There is no more miserable human being than one in whom nothing is habitual but indecision, and for whom the lighting of every cigar, the drinking of every cup, the time of rising and going to bed every day, and the beginning of every bit of work, are subjects of express volitional deliberation. Full half the time of such a man goes to the deciding, or regretting, of matters which ought to be so ingrained in him as practically not to exist for his consciousness at all."

(2) "In the acquisition of a new habit, or the leaving off of an old one, we must take care to launch ourselves with as strong and decided an initiative as possible. Accumulate all the possible circumstances which shall re-enforce the right motives ; put yourself assiduously in conditions that encourage the new way ; make engagements incompatible with the old ; take a public pledge, if the case allows ; in short, envelop your resolution with every aid you know. This will give your new beginning such a momentum that the temptation to break down will not occur as soon as it otherwise might ; and every day during which a breakdown is postponed adds to the chances of its not occurring at all."

(3) "Never suffer an exception to occur till the new habit is securely rooted in your life. Each lapse

is like the letting fall of a ball of string which one is carefully winding up; a single slip undoes more than a great many turns will wind again. Continuity of training is the great means of making the nervous system act infallibly right. . . . It is necessary, above all things, in such a situation, never to lose a battle. Every gain on the wrong side undoes the effect of many conquests on the right. . . . The need of securing success at the outset is imperative. Failure at first is apt to dampen the energy of all future attempts, while past experience of success nerves one to future vigour."

(4) "Seize the very first possible opportunity to act on every resolution you make, and on every emotional prompting you may experience in the direction of the habits you aspire to gain. It is not in the moment of their forming, but in the moment of their producing motor effects, that resolves and aspirations contribute the new 'set' to the brain. . . . No matter how full a reservoir of maxims one may possess, and no matter how good one's sentiments may be, if one have not taken advantage of every concrete opportunity to act, one's character may remain entirely unaffected for the better. With mere good intentions, hell is proverbially paved."

Of the importance of habit in the moral life there can be no manner of doubt; but we must also remember that habits are, after all, mechanical modes of behaviour, and that a universe of beings all acting uniformly and habitually with the precision of clockwork would not really be a moral world. While, then, we recognise the significance of habit,

THE MORAL SELF

and the help it may give in the conduct of life, we must repeat that habits are morally valuable only in so far as they contribute to the maintenance of the distinctive individuality of the self.

§ 5. **Some Educational Aspects of the Development of Personality.** The great educational maxim is that the individuality of the child should be respected, and should be allowed full scope for development. We all know that the aim of education is not to turn out children all of the same brand, as the factory turns out sewing-machines or type-writers. When education is so much standardised as it is, there is grave danger that it may tend to turn the children into human machines. The child's natural tendency to initiate, to invent, and to originate, may be repressed from the beginning. Education may end, after passing children through successive "standards," simply in producing dull mediocrity. To a considerable extent, this has happened in Germany, where education is excessively systematised.

(1) All the great educators have emphasised the importance of preserving and developing the child's individuality, and of adapting education to the child's individual needs. Thus Locke says, "Each man's mind has some peculiarity, as well as his face, that distinguishes him from all others; and there are possibly scarce two children who can be conducted by exactly the same method."[1] Even Herbart, with all his emphasis on the transforming power of education, insists that the individuality of the child which develops under the teacher's efforts should be respected and allowed as far as possible

[1] *Some Thoughts on Education*, § 216.

to follow its own bent.[1] Froebel claimed that from its earliest days the child should be given every opportunity to develop spontaneously its own individuality. For Froebel, the child's individuality is a sort of divine spark which should be allowed to conform to its own inner law.[2] And more recently Montessori has urged that the child's personality possesses a mysterious sanctity, which should never be invaded by the teacher. The teacher should beware of marring or stifling the mysterious powers which are latent in the self.[3]

(2) But while it is right that the child's individuality should be respected, it is well to remember that the individuality of the child is a growing thing. The child's individuality grows by what it feeds on. And it has to be recognised that it does not always desire what is best for it to feed on. The natural impulses of the child are not always worthy. Its tendencies may be perverted. The development of personality cannot always be allowed to proceed spontaneously. While the teacher must always respect the child's self, that self needs to be advised, to be guided, to be influenced, and to be directed.

(3) In this process of influencing and being influenced, the personalities of teacher and child come into contact. We sometimes forget that the teacher has an individuality as well as the child. As an influence on character, the teacher's personality may be of immense importance. What has been said with regard to respecting the child's individuality is

[1] Cf. *Science of Education*, bk. i. ch. ii.
[2] Cf. *The Education of Man*, §§ 7 and 8.
[3] Cf. *The Montessori Method*, ch. v.

perfectly consistent with the claim that the teacher should influence the child. For influence means that the personality of the child develops in response to the personality of the teacher. The personality of the child is not suppressed when he is influenced. The child is not driven : he is influenced ; he is attracted ; and his individuality is elicited. The teacher should not impose his personality upon the child, but he cannot help bringing it into contact with the child. Personality counts for much everywhere : but nowhere does it count for more than in education.

For further reading : G. F. Stout : *Manual*, bk. iv. ch. vii. ; W. James : *Principles*, vol. i. ch. iv. and x. ; J. Adams : *The Evolution of Educational Theory*, pp. 33-40 ; J. Dewey : *Educational Essays*, ch. i. and ii. ; M. Montessori : *The Montessori Method* ; F. Froebel : *The Education of Man*.

CHAPTER VII.

WILL AND CONSCIENCE.

§ 1. **The Self as Purposive and Regulative.** This chapter has been entitled "Will and Conscience," but we must begin by pointing out that will and conscience must not be regarded as separate faculties and powers. We often speak as if "will" and "conscience" were separate faculties with an existence and activity of their own apart from the self. "My conscience pricked me when I told that lie." "His will was too weak to prevent him yielding to the temptation to gamble." Thus we commonly distinguish the will and the conscience from the self, and we attribute to them an independent existence and independent activity. But this is quite wrong.

In reality, "will" and "conscience" are simply names which are given to certain aspects of the one self which is present in all mental behaviour and all moral conduct. We may consider the one self in different aspects and from various standpoints. We may consider it, in the first place, as purposive, as conative, as active. This is the self regarded as will. Or we may think of it as regulative, as reflective, as judicial. This is the self regarded as con-

WILL AND CONSCIENCE   101

science. But though these aspects differ, they are aspects of the *one* self. Suppose a man has an impulse to tell a " white lie," and suppose that he succeeds in restraining it. We may say that his conscience told him that the impulse was wrong, and his will prevented it issuing in action. But what has really happened is that he has brought the impulse into relation to his self as a whole. His self as reflective and judicial judges that the impulse is wrong, and his self as conative and active restrains it. In the former aspect the self functions as conscience, in the latter as will. But in both cases it is one and the same self.

We have already seen that the self sometimes seems divided against itself. A lower self may conflict with a higher. The business self may be discordant with the religious self. Now, in all cases of moral conflict between these different selves, the highest and best self is identified with will and conscience. This is the self which we like to regard as the *true* self. Thus, when we say, " My conscience pricked me when I told that lie," we would excuse ourselves by explaining, " I was not quite myself when I did it." The self which told the lie is not considered to be the true self. The conscience that pricked is the real self. Similarly, when we say, " His will was too weak to restrain him from gambling," we might apologise for him on the same grounds, " He was not quite himself when the sudden temptation came to him." His will is identified with his real self. But at the time his real self or will was not strong enough to overcome the sudden temptation. In every case where we commonly distinguish between will and conscience and the self, will and conscience are identified with the true self. By "will" and "conscience," then, we understand the self as conative and as regulative. Having premised this, we may now proceed to examine in some detail the nature of will and conscience respectively.

§ 2. **The Nature of Volition.** Volition must be distinguished from desire and from wish. (1) In a former chapter we saw that desires frequently conflict, and that only one of the conflicting desires can issue in action. The desire that issues in action, if organised in the self as a whole and acknowledged as its desire, is willed. The other desire is rejected as being alien to the true self. The self acknowledges one desire as its own, it throws itself upon its side, it "backs" it, it undertakes as far as in it lies to secure the attainment of the end that is desired; and thus the desire becomes definitely willed. It is a volition, and the actions in which it results are voluntary. The self always accepts responsibility for its volitions. When an action is willed by me, it is *my* action, and I am willing to stand by it. But I may look upon some of my mere desires as foreign to my real self, and may even regard them with horror and loathing.

(2) Volition also differs from mere wish. The distinction cannot be stated better than it was by Aristotle in his *Ethics*. "Nor yet can will be the same as wish, though it is evidently near akin to it. There can be no willing of impossibilities, and, if a man were to say that he willed something impossible, he would be thought a fool. But we wish for impossibilities as well as possibilities. Again, we

WILL AND CONSCIENCE

wish for things that could not possibly be performed by our agency, as, for instance, that a certain actor or a certain athlete should win the prize ; but no one wills anything of that sort : we only will things that we think may possibly be effected by our agency. Further, wish is mainly directed to the end and will to the means ; we wish to be in good health and we will the means of attaining good health. Or again, we wish to be happy, and we say so ; but it is inappropriate to say that we will to be happy, for, to put it generally, will appears to be confined to things in our power."[1]

It is one of the conditions of moral progress that we should not allow desires and wishes to remain mere desires and mere wishes. They should be brought into relation to the self as a whole. The self should judge whether they are worthy to be identified with itself or not. If it decides that they are worthy, it should "back" the desires so that they become volitions ; and, so far as the ends which it wishes are attainable, it should will the means by which they may be achieved. On the other hand, if desires are unworthy and wishes vain, they should at once be suppressed and denied. It is a source of weakness to the moral life to dally for a moment with desires which are evil or alien to the true self. And the weakest thing in the world is a life which is at the mercy of a swarm of impotent wishes. Like gnats, they goad it not to action but simply to irritation.

All volition involves deliberation on the one hand, and choice or decision on the other.

[1] Aristotle : *Ethics*, III. ii. §§ 7-9.

(1) It is always the self that deliberates. It asks, "Should *I* do this?" and "Should *I* do that?" In deliberation alternatives are brought before the self. These alternatives may simply be doing the action and leaving it undone. Or the alternatives may be conflicting desires. In the latter case the desires are brought into relation to the self as a whole, and the self deliberates which of the desires can most worthily be identified with itself. "The hackneyed example of moral deliberation is the case of an habitual drunkard under temptation. He has made a resolve to reform, but is now solicited again by the bottle. His moral triumph or failure literally consists in finding the right *name* for the case. If he says that it is a case of not wasting good liquor already poured out, or a case of not being churlish and unsociable when in the midst of friends, or a case of learning something at last about a brand of whisky he never met before, or a case of celebrating a public holiday, or a case of stimulating himself to a more energetic resolve in favour of abstinence than any he has ever yet made, then he is lost. His choice of the wrong name seals his doom. But if, in spite of all the plausible good names with which his thirsty fancy so copiously furnishes him, he unwaveringly clings to the truer bad name, and apperceives the case as that of 'being a drunkard, being a drunkard, being a drunkard,' his feet are planted on the road to salvation. He saves himself by thinking rightly."[1] Or, as Professor Stout puts it, "The thought of *getting drunk* attracts the man; but the thought of *his* getting drunk

[1] James: *Talks to Teachers*, pp. 187-188.

WILL AND CONSCIENCE

repels."[1] Thus, if we would deliberate well, we should always bring the possible courses of action into relation to the self as a whole. The question is not, "Do I desire this glass?" It is, "Do I desire myself as a person who has drunk this glass with *all* its consequences?"

(2) Eventually, however long the process of deliberation may last, one alternative is chosen. Henceforth this alternative becomes identified with the self. We have come to a decision, and we hold to it. "The most obvious difference between the state of indecision and that of decision is that in the first we do not know what we are going to do, and that in the second we do know what we are going to do. While deliberating, we are making up our mind, and we do not know what our mind is going to be. When we have formed a decision we have come to know our own minds. The conception of the self has become fixed where it was previously indeterminate. The realisation of one line of conative tendency is now definitely anticipated as part of our future life-history, so far at least as external conditions will allow of its execution."[2]

§ 3. **The Training of the Will.** It is of the utmost importance that the child should be trained to stand by his decisions. It is, indeed, often very much easier to maintain our decisions than to arrive at them. But it may on occasion be very difficult to remain true to our choice. More particularly is this the case when the decision was a noble one which involved self-sacrifice. The man who has chosen

[1] Stout: *Manual of Psychology*, p. 708.
[2] *Ibid.* p. 710.

the straight and narrow path is often tempted to abandon it. "Tasks in hours of insight willed may be through hours of gloom fulfilled." But, in general, a decision once formed tends to maintain itself. Three reasons for this have been given by Professor Stout.

(1) "When I judge that in so far as in me lies I shall realise a certain end, the endeavour to realise that end becomes *ipso facto* an integral part of the conception of myself. Failure to realise it is regarded as *my* failure, *my* defeat. Thus volition becomes strengthened in the face of obstacles by all the combative emotions. These are of varying kinds and of varying degrees of strength in different individuals; but all tendencies to hold out or to struggle against opposition, merely because it *is* opposition, are enlisted in the service of the will, inasmuch as the idea of the line of conduct willed is an integral part of the idea of self." [1]

(2) "The fixity of the will is also strengthened, often in a very high degree, by aversion to the state of irresolution. Suspense is in itself disagreeable; and when we have emerged from it by a voluntary decision, we shrink from lapsing into it once more. Besides this, prolonged and repeated indecision is highly detrimental in the general conduct of life. The man who knows his own mind is far more efficient than the man who is always wavering. Hence, in most persons there is a strong tendency to abide by a resolution, just because it *is* a resolution. This tendency is greatly strengthened by social relations. If we are weak and vacillating, no one will depend

[1] *Mind*, N.S., vol. v. p. 358.

WILL AND CONSCIENCE

on us ; we shall be viewed with a kind of contempt. Mere vanity may go far to give fixity to the will "[1]

(3) " Volition also becomes fixed by the action which follows on it. So soon as we have attained the settled belief that we are going to follow out a certain line of conduct, we immediately begin to adapt our thoughts and deeds to this belief. We thus come to be more and more *committed* to the course determined on. To withdraw from it would be to disturb our arrangements ; to baulk expectations raised in others ; and to arrest the general flow of our own mental activity. The more the mind has become set on one thing, the more it would be upset by being diverted to another."[2]

These three points are so important that they may be epitomised in three ethical maxims. (1) Immediately identify with your self the course of action decided upon. (2) Avoid relapsing into irresolution. (3) Translate your decision into action at the earliest possible moment.

§ 4. **Some Educational Aspects.** It follows from all this that there is eternal truth in such copy-book maxims as " Perseverance is a Virtue " and " If at first you don't succeed, try, try, try again." The triteness of these hackneyed precepts often blinds us to their truth. Yet there is no moral lesson which the child needs to learn more than this. It is not natural for the child to persevere. Its purposes are short-lived, just as its desires are transient and its ideals partial. It very soon tires of trying to do what is unpleasant or uninteresting.

[1] *Op. cit.* p. 359.
[2] *Manual of Psychology*, p. 716.

And it is not without pain that it learns the lesson of perseverance. Organised games are one of the most useful educational means of teaching the child to persist in what he is doing. The boy knows that he must " stick in " and not " slack it," if he wants to get into the school team. On the playing-field he realises that perseverance *is* a virtue, and he ought then to be more ready to be persuaded to cultivate this virtue in relation to his school work. Here, indeed, perseverance is more difficult, because it is necessary to concentrate the attention on the uninteresting task. And the attention of the child, like the attention of most adults, is a very uncertain thing, which comes only by fits and starts. But the child *can* learn to form habits of concentrated attention. Such habits are formed only by perseverance in recalling the wandering mind to the subject in hand. Perseverance is entirely an affair of the will.

The exercise of will is not an easy thing. Most people whose time is largely at their own disposal know how readily they relapse into a state of *aboulia*, or simple incapacity to will. A man lies in bed on a summer morning, simply because he cannot get himself to will to rise. He knows he ought to be up. He knows that the morning is bright and warm. He knows he will be just as comfortable after his bath and breakfast as he is in bed. He may revolve all these thoughts in his mind. Yet he cannot will to rise. It is precisely because it is often so hard to will simple actions that it is so important to form good habits in accordance with which we shall act habitually without needing to will the action on every occasion. The man who forms the habit of rising at the same hour saves not only much time but much nervous strain. For it is a strain to know that one ought to do a thing, and yet feel unable to will it. And such an incapacity to will what we know we ought to do, if indulged in such a small affair as lying a-bed of a morning, is apt to appear in a very startling way when much graver matters are at stake.

Willed action is often " in the line of greatest resistance." We have to overcome obstacles to the attainment of some ideal end, and our inclination would lead us to turn aside from this difficult task and follow the line of least resistance. But we know that we *ought* to act in obedience to the ideal, however rough the path may be. Most willed action involves a struggle. There is a saying of the Greek sage Pittacus, which deserves to be inscribed in letters of gold in every schoolroom and in every home : " It is *hard* to be good."

'It is " hard to be good " because—to mention one reason—it is often difficult to *will* to do what we ought to do. So far, we have been assuming that we *know* what we ought to do. But the difficulty of being good is sometimes due to our ignorance what really is the right thing to do. Now, it is the function of the self, acting as conscience, to tell us what is and what is not the right thing to do. We must therefore go on to ask what exactly we mean by conscience, and what is its place in the moral life.

§ 5. **The Meaning of Conscience.** There are two mistaken views of conscience, which are so commonly held, that it is impossible to pass them over in silence. Each of these theories has been maintained by eminent philosophers, and a line or two must be devoted to stating and criticising them.

The first view is that at which we glanced at the beginning of the chapter. The theory that conscience is a separate faculty of the mind was strongly defended by Bishop Butler, one of the most honoured names in the history of English Ethics. Butler says that conscience is a faculty of peculiar sanctity, in kind and nature supreme over all others. This faculty, which is purely rational, has absolute and unquestioned authority. It passes judgment both on the man and his actions. It pronounces without the possibility of error, and without the possibility of appeal, that some actions are in themselves right, just, and good, and that others are in themselves evil, wrong, and unjust. It is a "magisterial faculty," whose prerogative it is to judge and govern, with perfect impartiality and perfect authority.

Now, in answer to this, we must point out (a) that psychology has now established that there are no separate and distinct faculties of the mind, and therefore an isolated moral faculty or conscience is simply a fiction. (b) The peculiar "sanctity" of conscience comes, not from conscience itself, but from the kind of objects with which the self is concerned in making moral judgments. Moral judgments are made with regard to the good and duty, and it is these which have a special sanctity.

According to the other view, conscience is simply a group of instincts, or a collection of emotions, or an aggregate of sentiments—in short, a bundle of feelings. Conscience is of the heart, not of the head. It is simply the conglomeration of feelings which makes us feel good when we do right, and feel bad when we do wrong.[1]

In criticism of this view, we may urge (a) that feelings do not have the permanence that conscience possesses. Feelings are capricious and uncertain, varying from moment to moment. But conscience is constant and systematic. (b) Feelings are not reflective. Feelings give an immediate sense of value, but they cannot reflect on themselves or on anything else. But conscience is reflective. The fact that it often does not " prick " till after the action has been performed shows that its verdict is based on reflection.

But though both of these views as they stand are erroneous, they each contain an element of truth. (1) It is true that conscience is rational. Conscience is the self making moral judgments. And judgment is always rational. Conscience is often pictured as a kind of judge. It carries on judicial investigation, it accuses, it bears witness, and it passes sentence. In all these judicial operations the rational aspect of conscience is prominent. Conscience is simply intelligence occupied with a certain kind of subject-matter. Conscientious reflection is distinguished from reflection in general, not as a special kind of mental activity ; but as dealing with a special class of objects. When intelligence deals with the rela-

[1] Varieties of this view have been maintained by Shaftesbury and Hutcheson, and by Hume, Mill, and Leslie Stephen ; and more recently by Prof. Westermarck (*The Origin and Development of the Moral Ideas*) and Dr. M'Dougall (*Social Psychology*).

tions of persons and moral actions, it is called conscience. Conscience is, indeed, simply consciousness dealing with moral life.

(2) But conscience also includes feeling. When conscience judges that such and such an action is wrong, we immediately feel that it is wrong. If my conscience judges that an action which I have committed is wrong, I immediately feel remorse. In addition to this, all moral judgments involve some emotional accompaniments. All moral judgments deal with moral conduct, and however impartial the judgment purports to be, it is always accompanied by the feelings natural to our attitude to the person or persons whose conduct is being judged. Our liking or dislike, our friendship or coolness, our love or hatred for a man will, however hard we try to exclude them, tinge the judgments we pass on his conduct.

Both reason and feeling are comprehended within the self. And conscience is the whole self, as reasoning and feeling, as estimating the rightness and wrongness of actions, in accordance with some moral standard, and with reference to some moral ideal, as sympathising with the various motives which influence it, and as weighing the consequences that will probably follow from its actions. Conscience is simply the moral aspect of personality or self-consciousness. The man's whole personality, when he engages in moral action or makes a moral judgment, is his conscience.

§ 6. **Conflicts of Conscience.** Conflicts may occur within the conscience itself. Conscience may not be harmonious. It may not be consistent in its judg-

WILL AND CONSCIENCE

ments. The self is rarely developed equally completely on every side. So the conscience may often be unduly callous in one direction, and excessively sensitive in another. One man's conscience may be exceedingly punctilious in insisting on the exact letter of religious observance, though he may have no scruple whatever in engineering commercial enterprises of doubtful morality. Another man may be thoroughly dishonest in business, and yet be exemplary in his domestic relations. These are no doubt extreme instances; but we all know people whose consciences would repudiate indignantly a temptation to steal, and yet passively acquiesce in an attempt to defraud a railway company. Such inconsistencies in the judgments of the individual conscience indicate that the self has not been perfectly unified. If it were completely harmonised, its judgments would always be absolutely consistent.

Conflicts may also take place between the conscience of one man and the conscience of his neighbour, or between one man's conscience and the public or universal conscience. The law of the land may command certain actions which an individual regards as immoral, or a man's country may be engaged in a war which he believes unjust. Is he, in the first case, to obey the State and disobey his own conscience by performing the act that is enjoined? In the second, should he stifle the judgment of his conscience, and pay taxes to maintain the war or contribute his personal services to it? Is he to hearken to the voice of his private conscience or that of the State? In such a conflict a man should always suspect the rightness of the judgment of his private conscience. It is just possible that his conscience may be, in Ruskin's phrase, "the conscience of an ass." Or he may be taking for the verdict of conscience what is simply an unexamined prejudice. A man has no right to a private conscience in any matter which he has not taken pains to understand. A man's first duty, then, is to examine the judgment of his conscience, and to make quite certain that he has acquired sufficient knowledge of the question at issue. But if he is satisfied, after full reflection on all the circumstances, that the verdict of his private conscience is right, then he must at all costs obey it.

§ 7. **The Education of Conscience.** The aim of the education of conscience is the removal of such conflicts as these. In an ideal condition of society each man's conscience would function always and everywhere consistently with itself, and harmoniously with the public or universal conscience. With a view to such an ideal as this, how is conscience to be educated?

(1) The individual conscience should be organised harmoniously. In other words, the self as a whole should be systematised in an all-round development, in which each aspect of the self is allowed an opportunity to grow. Thus it should be possible to do something to overcome the tendency of conscience to be slack in some directions, and excessively scrupulous in others. Here, as everywhere else, a harmonious moral life depends on the development of the self in accordance with a comprehensive and worthy moral ideal.

(2) Conscience must be enlightened. Ethics rests on the assumption that if all men had the same

knowledge, their moral judgments would be in perfect agreement. Unless men have a certain stock of knowledge, reflection is either impossible or futile. In order that our moral judgments may be sound we must have knowledge.

(3) If men have adequate knowledge and form habits of reflecting before acting, their consciences will function *before* action instead of after. As it is, in the case of many men, the sting or prick of conscience comes too late : it is not felt till after the action has been done, and the only remedy then may be a vain remorse. Thus we often hear those who suddenly realise the sinfulness or wrongness of their conduct exclaim, " I never *thought*," " If I had only *thought* ! " If conscience had pronounced the action wrong before it was done, it would probably never have been performed. Therefore let reflection precede action : " Look before you leap."

(4) Of course, there is a danger here. A man may look so long that he will never leap. But in such cases reflection has been indulged until it has become morbid. It has become an introspective inquisition of the depths of one's own moral life. And such self-examination is apt, in addition to weakening the springs of conduct, to turn men into canting prigs. But it is possible to avoid this result. There is such a thing as an honest conscientiousness. Conscientiousness is simply the formed habit of bringing conscience or intelligence to bear upon the actual moral situations in which we daily find ourselves. Hence the ethical and educational maxim : So train the child to refer his moral difficulties to the judgment of his conscience, that he will gradually come

to develop a conscientious character, which will habitually judge of the moral worth of his thoughts and actions.

For further reading : (on Will) G. F. Stout : *Manual*, bk. iv., ch. x. ; W. James : *Talks to Teachers*, ch. xv. ; J. Burnet : *Aristotle on Education*, pp. 66-83 ; J. Dewey : *Educational Essays*, ch. ii. ; (on Conscience) J. H. Muirhead : *Elements of Ethics*, §§ 31-35, 97-98 ; S. E. Mezes : *Ethics*, ch. vi.-viii. ; Butler : *Sermons*, i. and ii. ; A. E. Taylor : *The Problem of Conduct*, pp. 147-152.

PART II.

THE REALISATION OF CHARACTER IN VOCATION.

CHAPTER VIII.

CHARACTER AND CONDUCT.

§ 1. **The Growth of Character.** In Part I. we traced the development of character, and examined in detail the various elements which go to constitute it. We found that the ultimate groundwork of character is provided by heredity, but that this groundwork would remain simply a formless aggregate of blind tendencies and empty capacities, if the environment were not allowed to influence it. We considered the influence of the physical and social environment on the development of the early life of the child, and showed how the rudimentary instincts with which the child starts are modified and developed to form the basis of the great institutions of the moral life. Then, along two main lines, we traced the development of character out of the purely instinctive tendencies of human life. We showed that impulses, which may be regarded as instincts in their active or executive aspect, may be controlled and developed into desires, which are relatively permanent and pervasive. Again, emotions, which in their origin appear at the instinctive level of life, may be organised into systematic sentiments, which colour the whole moral life. But comprehensive as these desires and sentiments are, they may yet lead to conflict and disharmony in the moral life, unless they are unified in a permanent and self-conscious personality. Only then do we reach the level of formed character, for character is the moral self. We then considered the self or character in relation to practical life, first as willing its actions, and second as judging its own and other people's thoughts and actions. Will and conscience, we saw, are necessarily involved in character. Character is the moral self as a whole, as comprehending and organising, with the help of habit, all the processes that take place within it, and as co-ordinating and harmonising all the actions in which it expresses itself.

§ 2. **The Relation of Character to Conduct.** So far we have been concerned with the self and its processes rather than with the actions in which it manifests its activity, with its capacities and tendencies rather than with the actual behaviour in which they are realised. In a word, we have been studying the character of the self rather than its conduct. We must now ask, How is character related to conduct? The relation is a double one.

On the one hand, character determines conduct. Conduct consists of human actions, and these are always regarded as the expressions of the character of the man whose actions they are. A man's actions

CHARACTER AND CONDUCT

are determined by his character, so that if his character be good his actions will also be good, and if his character be evil his actions will also be evil.[1] His conduct flows from his character, and is an index to it. In ordinary life we always assume—and we are perfectly right to do so—that a man's conduct reveals his character. In practice all our estimates of people's characters are based on what we know of their conduct. If we did not assume that conduct is determined by character, we could pass no moral judgments on the characters of others. We believe

---

[1] This is true on the whole. But many exceptions to the general rule may occur. Men of good character often do wrong, and men of evil character may do noble actions. But normally, in general, good character will issue in right actions. If a man acts inconsistently with his character, this may be explained in three ways:

(1) The self may not be completely systematised and unified. We may call the character good on the whole, though there may be aspects of the self which are not in harmony with the self as a whole. Hence isolated actions may be performed which are wrong and inconsistent with the character as a whole. Most people would agree that on the whole Queen Victoria's character was good, though some of her actions were undoubtedly wrong.

(2) A good man may do wrong because of inadequate knowledge. His wrong action is due to intellectual error, and not to voluntary sin. He is very often held responsible for his action, and he may even blame himself bitterly for it, but such an action is not really an expression of his character, unless his ignorance was due to culpable negligence.

(3) A good man may do wrong in a sudden gust of passion. Some overwhelming impulse may issue in action before he can marshal his moral strength to restrain it. In such cases a man is justly held responsible for his action on the ground that he ought to have been able to resist the temptation and control the impulse. But such an action is not really an expression of character. The man's character disclaims the impulsive action. "How could I have done it?" he asks himself afterwards. The action does not really reveal the character, at least in any positive way. What it does is to indicate a weakness in the character.

that if we could have a complete record of a man's conduct in every department of life and at every stage in life—through childhood, youth, manhood, and old age, as son, brother, husband, and father, as an inferior, superior, and equal, in friendship and enmity, at work and play, in prosperity and adversity, as a citizen of a State and a member of a Church—we should have a complete expression of his character. We assume that all his actions have been produced by his character.

On the other hand, conduct determines character. As we have seen, character is not something absolutely fixed. Character is a growing system; it is in constant process of growth; and its development is influenced by the kind of actions it habitually performs. Every one of a self's actions has some effect, however infinitesimal, on the formation of its character. Aristotle constantly insists that a man acquires a good or bad character by the habitual repetition of good or bad actions. Training and habituation in the performance of actual good actions are necessary for the production of a good character. We start simply with capacities. Now, the capacity for being good is the same thing as the capacity for being bad. Every child is born with an infinite capacity for good or evil, and it depends on training and habituation in which of the two ways the capacities will become realised as character. "It is by doing just acts that we become just, by doing temperate acts that we become temperate, and by doing brave deeds that we become brave." [1] In this sense, conduct determines character.

[1] Aristotle: *Ethics*, II. i. § 4.

§ 3. **The Meaning of Conduct.** It follows from the close connection of character and conduct that there is a certain constancy and consistency in conduct. The educated man's conduct does not consist of isolated actions occurring at haphazard with no bond of unity or tie of purpose. His conduct displays a certain uniformity ; it is *his* conduct and he acknowledges it and stands by it. We may define conduct as self-conscious behaviour, or as the system of a man's voluntary actions. What precisely this definition implies will become clear if we distinguish conduct from actions in general and from behaviour in general.

(1) Conduct consists in actions. But not all actions constitute conduct. We speak of the action of a motor-car or a sewing-machine or a type-writer. But we should not dream of talking of their conduct. Mechanical action is not conduct. Nor is all human action conduct. Certain human actions, *e.g.* reflex actions, are really mechanical. They take place naturally and necessarily in response to a particular external stimulus, in just as mechanical a way as the type-writer prints a letter when the key is depressed. Conduct consists only in voluntary human actions.

(2) Conduct is behaviour. But not all behaviour is conduct. We speak of the behaviour of the lower animals. The physiologist studies the behaviour of the frogs on which he experiments. But we do not ascribe conduct to the lower animals. Conduct is self-conscious behaviour. Conduct involves self-consciousness ; and no animal is self-conscious. Self-consciousness implies the capacity to represent to oneself some end or aim, and to will the course of

action necessary to attain that end. The self-conscious person is able to propose to himself, as an aim to be achieved by himself, something which he regards as worth while, and to plan and carry through the line of action by which the end will be realised.

§ 4. **The Implications of Conduct: Freedom, Responsibility, Obligation, and Value.** Some important consequences follow from this conception of conduct.

(1) Conduct implies freedom. This, indeed, has been assumed in all we have said about the relation of character and conduct. We simply took it for granted that a man's character expresses itself freely in his actions. Conduct could not be an index to character unless it were free. Human conduct is free, both positively and negatively. Man is free from the dominion of particular impulses and appetites. The animal is governed by his appetites and impulses, but man is emancipated from the slavery they would fain impose. Man is able, as we have seen, to consider his impulses and desires, his emotions and sentiments, in relation to his self and the comprehensive ideals which he cherishes ; and he can reject, restrain, modify, confirm, or encourage them as he wills. In all his conduct man should be realising his highest individuality : his conduct is free and spontaneous.

(2) All conduct is responsible conduct. Man's moral responsibility is a consequence of his freedom. If all man's actions were mechanically produced, like those of the steam engine or electric dynamo, he could not be held accountable for them. The steam engine is not responsible for its breakdowns. The responsibility for them is shifted on to the shoulders

CHARACTER AND CONDUCT

of the engineer. A bull is not held responsible if he gores a child. The responsibility for the bull's acts is referred to its owner. In every case responsibility attaches to the character of a human being. Man acknowledges his conduct as his own and accepts responsibility for it.[1]

(3) Conduct involves moral obligation. Every action is either right or wrong. Right conduct is conduct that ought to be as it is; and wrong conduct is conduct that ought not to be as it is. Of every moral action we can say either that it ought to have been done, or that it ought not to have been done. An ideal of duty is implied in all conduct. Now, moral obligation attaches only to conduct. I cannot strictly say that my type-writer *ought* to run more smoothly than it does: no moral obligation can attach to it: the type-writer has no duty. If I do say that it ought to work more smoothly, what I really mean is that the makers ought to have built it more carefully, or that I ought to have kept it free from dust. The *ought* is really referred from the type-writer to some person who is responsible for it.

(4) All conduct is conceived to have some moral value. The moral quality of conduct depends partly on the disposition and attitude of the self whose conduct it is. This disposition will comprise feelings of pleasure and pain, and certain emotions and

[1] That only human beings are responsible agents is a principle that took long to establish. According to the Mosaic code, an ox which gored a man was to be put to death (Ex. xxi. 28). During the Middle Ages, pigs, rats, and other animals were prosecuted before the civil and ecclesiastical courts. Thus, in 1403 in Paris a pig was tried, condemned, and executed for the murder of a baby. Animals were thought to be both morally and legally responsible.

sentiments. The value of conduct is partly estimated in terms of satisfaction and dissatisfaction, of happiness and misery.

§ 5. **Conduct and the School.** It is often maintained that the life of the child in school is highly artificial, and that the ordinary school curriculum affords little opportunity to the child to develop qualities of character that it will need in later life. According to this argument, the child's character at school issues in departments of conduct which are quite other than those which express its life in the outer world. Now, there are, of course, obvious differences between the life that the child lives in school and the life that he lives outside and will live after his schooldays are over. And in spite of all that has been done and advocated by Froebel and Montessori—to mention only two names—to minimise this difference and secure for the child a more natural school-life, it is certain that, from the nature of the case, school-life must continue to differ in some respects from the rest of the child's life. But it does not follow that the conduct of the child in school is something so utterly different from the rest of its conduct that the training it receives in school will have no influence on the formation of its character as a whole. On the contrary, if we train children in those aspects of conduct which manifest themselves in the life of the class-room or playing-fields, that training should normally influence the development of the character as a whole. Thus, even those departments of conduct which are not touched by ordinary school-life will be affected by the training received in school, for that education will influence the whole character, from which every voluntary act issues. In particular, it may be shown that every one of the implications of conduct, whose importance has been indicated, is present in the ordinary conduct of the child at school.

(1) The child is free in his activities. He requires, of course, to submit to discipline, but educationists have insisted, on the whole with singular unanimity, that he should be made to feel that the authority to which he is subjected is not alien to himself, but is the condition of his own highest development; that he should be encouraged to maintain discipline in class and in play by himself; and that, so far as possible, he should be encouraged to develop his own individuality spontaneously along the lines most natural and congenial to himself.

(2) The notion of responsibility is strongly developed in the conduct of the child at school. He is held responsible for everything he does. He is responsible for every class task he performs, and he receives credit or blame accordingly. He is regarded as responsible for his punctuality and attendance, unless his parents expressly acknowledge by " note " that they accept responsibility for it. As the child grows older, he may be made responsible for the conduct of others. As monitor or prefect or captain of a games team his responsibility may be considerable, and to him may even seem oppressive. The lesson of responsibility is one that the child learns pre-eminently at school.

(3) The child's school-life is saturated with moral obligation. The danger is not that this aspect of school-life should be absent, but that it should be

too constantly and too intensely present. The child naturally regards his school tasks as duties, and he recognises that he is under an obligation to discharge them. But too often the duties seem wholly disagreeable, and the obligation appears to be externally imposed by a grim authority. The consequence is that the notion of duty is apt to be defined in the child's mind as "that which is unpleasant" or "that which is to be avoided if at all possible." Such early associations of duty may do lifelong harm to the child by making it impossible for him to see that his duty may be at the same time his highest privilege and his truest pleasure. And moral progress depends on learning that lesson.

(4) It follows from what has just been said that the value-aspect of conduct is often inadequately developed in schools. Vast numbers of children pass through our schools without ever realising, without ever feeling, the sense of value in connection with their education. Their one desire is to be free of the drudgery of school at the earliest possible moment. Their education seems to have no value-for-life for them. It is the great problem of education (a) so to organise the curriculum as to afford the greatest value-for-life for the child, and (b) so to present it to the child that he will *appreciate* its value.

For further reading: J. S. Mackenzie: *Manual*, bk. i. ch. iii.; J. H. Muirhead: *Elements*, §§ 15-20; J. Dewey and J. H Tufts: *Ethics*, ch. i. and xiii.; Aristotle: *Ethics*, bk. i. and ii.

CHAPTER IX.

THE STANDARD OF MORAL JUDGMENT.

§ 1. **The Development of Moral Judgment.** Moral judgments are passed by the self, acting as conscience, on conduct and character. The object that is judged is always a human action or a system of human actions. We have now to ask, What standard do we use when we make moral judgments on conduct?

Some standard is involved in every kind of judgment. The legal judgment pronounced by the judge is based on the enacted law of his country. When, in common life, we judge that a certain man is tall, we make our judgment with reference to some average height which we take to be the normal or standard height for a man. When we judge that a certain play is clever, we have in mind some standard of cleverness in relation to which we make our judgment. But, though we all constantly make such judgments, we should find it very difficult to define exactly what our standard is. How many people could state the average height of an Englishman, or define the standard of dramatic cleverness? We regularly use standards which we have never attempted to formulate.

The same thing is true of moral judgment. From our earliest years we have been making judgments on our own or other people's actions and character. We have called this man "good" and that one "bad," this action "right" and that one "wrong." These judgments all necessarily involve some standard. Yet very few people have reflected on the nature of this standard.

The best way to investigate the meaning of the standard is to trace the origin and growth of moral judgment in the child. As soon as the child becomes aware of the existence of persons, it begins to perceive that moral judgments are passed upon it by these other persons. Of course, it does not call them moral judgments, but it gradually comes to have a more and more distinct conception of the meaning of such a moral judgment as "Baby is naughty to cry for his bottle," "Baby ought to like his bath," "Baby has been a good boy this morning." Very soon baby begins to pass moral judgments himself. In taking this step he is influenced by the two fundamental characteristics which all children possess in some measure, the tendency to imitate, and the tendency to originate. The child imitates his elders in everything; he copies their language, their gestures, their actions, and even subtle nuances of character of which they may have been unconscious until they saw them mirrored in the child. The child also imitates the moral judgments that are passed upon him. The tendency to copy his parents' moral judgments is very marked if the child has a younger brother and sister. His parents tell him that he is naughty when he cries. Therefore he tells baby that *he* is naughty when he cries. The same moral judgment is passed on the same kind of action.

But the child also has a natural tendency to originate, to initiate, to invent. Hence he applies the moral judgments which he has learned by imitation to actions other than those to which they were originally attached. Nurse is naughty when she puts him to bed too early for his taste. Mother is naughty when she refuses to give him a biscuit. The child has originated these moral judgments. But he soon comes to realise that the moral judgments which he has originated do not seem to have the same validity as mother's moral judgments. When he cries, mother's moral judgment is, "You are naughty"; and if he persists, mother makes her judgment effective by whipping him. On the other hand, when he says to mother, "You are naughty," he cannot make his judgment effective, and if he tries to do so, mother passes the judgment "You are naughty" on him, and very soon makes this judgment effective. From such experiences as these, the child gradually learns that (1) when mother makes a judgment, it *is* so; (2) when he makes a judgment on his own initiative, it may not be valid; and (3) when he makes a judgment in strict imitation of mother's, *e.g.* upon baby crying, the moral judgment is sound. Hence he comes to accept mother's moral judgment as his standard.

§ 2. **The Standard as Private Opinion.** Now the moral judgments of the mother may be based simply on her private opinion. So long as the child comes in contact only with her private opinion, her judgments will have for him, as soon as he has realised the futility of his own independent judgments, the force of absolute law. But suppose one day mother makes a moral judgment, and father (also a being having authority) makes another, inconsistent with mother's, the child begins to suspect the soundness of mother's moral judgments. In a dim way he recognises that if, with regard to the same action, mother says he is naughty and father says he is good, both these moral judgments cannot be true. If such conflicts occur with any frequency, mother's moral judgments become degraded from the enactments of absolute law to (what they really are) the expressions of private opinion.

But the moral standard (we may say on behalf of the child) cannot be private opinion, because it would then follow that there is no such thing as right and wrong and good and bad. If the only standard of moral judgment were private opinion, then what I think right would be right for me, and no one could contradict me. If anyone did, I could retort, "That is only your opinion, and my opinion is as good as yours."

§ 3. **The Standard as Social Convention.** If the child should persistently try to exert his private opinion in opposition to the private opinions of his mother and father, he will find that father and mother will unite against him. On most points their opinions are in agreement, and in the normal home the child comes to realise that their attitude to him is in essentials the same, and that on the whole the moral judgments which they pass on him coincide. The standard of moral judgment is no longer simply private opinion: it is family-opinion, or group-opinion.

In most matters the child adopts the moral standards of his family or whatever social group is most prominent in his environment. If he comes in contact with more than one social group, he may find that the general standards which they employ differ in startling respects. But he will also become aware of an underlying agreement. As his parents' judgments differed in some respects but agreed in most, so the moral judgments of the various social groups differ in certain matters but are in general agreement. This underlying unity expresses itself in " public opinion " or " social convention."

Social convention supplies the standard to which most of the growing child's judgments conform. There is no more conventional creature than the adolescent. He adopts his manners and customs from current convention, he follows it with minute care in the colour of his tie and the way in which he parts his hair. In fashions and manners the boy and girl are exceedingly sensitive to its decrees. They would not dream of questioning its authority. In more distinctly moral matters, too, social convention seems to be the infallible criterion of goodness and badness. The youth condemns what the convention of his " set " condemns. A man is approved as a " ripper " or stigmatised as a " blighter," in accordance with this convention. Social convention becomes the only standard of moral judgment. The youth judges that a certain action, *e.g.* cheating at cards, is wrong, because social convention decrees that it is wrong.

But the youth often begins to doubt whether, after all, social convention is the ultimate criterion of good and evil. He sometimes feels a lurking suspicion that our social conventions may be all wrong. And if he reflects at all, and does not simply stifle his doubt and distrust, he will come to the conclusion that social convention is inadequate to supply the standard of moral judgment. And that for two reasons.

(1) Social conventions have only *local* validity. The conventions of one country differ from those of another. In many respects the conventional standards of Germany and Britain are very different. And we find even greater divergences if we compare the conventional standards of the Western world with those of the Orient. Now ethics demands that what is right in one place must be right under similar circumstances everywhere. The standard of moral judgment must be the same everywhere. Ethics can never rest in the fact that "there ain't no Ten Commandments" east of Suez. Ethics maintains that, if the Ten Commandments are a true expression of the moral standard, they must be true universally.

(2) Social conventions have only *temporary* validity. The conventions of one time differ from those of another. Moral conventions, it is true, do not usually change so rapidly and capriciously as those which determine fashions and manners. Yet they *do* change, and sometimes in a swift and arbitrary way. The moral conventions of the Commonwealth were very different from those of the Restoration, and those of mid-Victorian England varied in marked respects from those that hold at the present time.

Social convention does not have the permanence and stability necessary to constitute the standard of moral judgment.

§ 4. The Standard as Feeling. When the average man becomes impressed with the inadequacy of social convention as the standard of moral judgment, he may not have clearly present to his mind the definite reasons which we have just assigned for rejecting its claims. He may merely come to feel for it a deep-seated distrust, of which he can give no explanation. He simply *feels* that social convention is not a satisfactory standard. And he is apt to come to the conclusion that there is really no standard, and that his own feelings, in which alone he cannot be mistaken, supply the only working test of the value of his actions. He *feels* good when he treats generously a man who has injured him, he *feels* satisfied when he has done his duty in business, he *feels* a rush of compassion when he assists a penniless orphan, he *feels* bad when he tells a lie or cheats at cards, and he *feels* angry and disgusted when he allows laziness to overcome his conviction that he ought to be at work.

Further, especially if his nature be sympathetic, he will be affected in much the same way by the actions of others. He *feels* that the man who treats his enemy generously is good, and he *feels* that the man who tells lies and cheats at cards is bad. Thus he comes to feel moral approval for all actions of a certain kind, whether performed by him or by others; and moral disapproval for all actions of another kind, whether they are his own or somebody else's. For instance, he feels moral approval for all acts of conspicuous bravery, whether these deeds are done by himself or others ; and he has a feeling of moral disapprobation for all deliberate lies, whether they are told by him or by others. His moral judgment depends on his feeling-attitude. All actions for which he has a feeling of moral approval are right, and all actions for which he has a feeling of moral disapproval are wrong.

Now, at first sight, this standard seems a very simple one. We know when we have feelings of moral approbation or disapprobation, and therefore we shall always know which actions are right and which are wrong.

But a difficulty immediately arises. All men do not feel in the same way. I may feel strong moral *disapprobation* for a certain action, but your feeling of moral *approbation* may be equally strong. Many excellent people feel that it is always wrong for anybody to go to the theatre, but many excellent people feel that it is quite right. Now it is impossible for the same action to be at one and the same time both right and wrong : if it is right, it cannot be at the same time wrong ; and if it is wrong, it cannot be at the same time right. Yet, towards the same action, say A's going to the theatre, B feels moral approbation, and C feels moral disapproval. B bases his moral judgment on his feeling, and says that A's conduct is right : C bases his judgment on his feeling, and says that A's conduct is wrong. But A's conduct must be either right or wrong : it cannot be both right and wrong. Therefore either B's judgment or C's judgment is wrong, and consequently one of them must have been using a wrong standard. But each was using his own feeling as the standard. Now all moral judgments based on a true moral standard are consistent. Hence such conflicts as this show that feeling cannot be the moral standard.

Feeling is inadequate as the basis of moral judgment for two reasons. (1) Feelings are essentially private. A man's feelings are his, and though he can describe them to others, they cannot really share them. Men differ in nothing so much as their feelings. A man's feelings are secret: he knows that nobody in the world knows all about his feelings, and he cannot assume that he knows all about any other person's feelings. Now the standard of moral judgment must be public; it must be common to all men, and alike for all men.

(2) Feelings are essentially transient. A man's feelings are the most variable part of him. His whole feeling-attitude may change many times in a single day. Even his feelings of moral approval and disapproval, which are generally less capricious than the rest of his feeling-self, are affected by the sudden alterations that take place in his feeling-disposition. But, as we have already seen, the standard of moral judgment must be something constant, permanent, and consistent.

§ 5. **The Standard as Reason.** When we reflect, we see that moral judgment must be based on reason. Our moral judgments, in fact, are rational in precisely the same way as any of our other judgments. All judgment is rational, and moral judgments differ from all other judgments, not in the actual mental process of judging, but in the object of the judgment. Moral judgment is simply ordinary judgment on the special subject-matter of conduct. The standard of moral judgment is not immediately given in private feeling or opinion or intuition, nor crystallised in social convention or law. It needs to be reflected on and reasoned about. Moral judgment is rational, and the standard it employs must be investigated by a process of reasoning.

The dependence of moral judgment on reason will become clear, if we bear in mind certain general characteristics, which belong to all true moral judgment.

(1) All true moral judgments are *objective*. They are judgments upon actions, and not upon people's feelings or opinions with regard to those actions. When we make the moral judgment that Cromwell did wrong when he sacked Drogheda, we are making a judgment about Cromwell's action as an object. We do not merely mean that we have certain feelings towards Cromwell : we mean that on rational grounds, of which we can give a reasonable account, we definitely judge that his action was wrong. Moral judgments are objective : they are not simply the expression of private likes and dislikes.

(2) Moral judgments imply *universality*. True moral judgments are universally true. Of course, we may make mistakes in our moral judgments, just as we may make mistakes in other departments of rational activity. But in these cases we recognise that we have made a mistake, and that there is a definite and universal right and wrong. If a long multiplication sum be given out to a class of small boys, the answers they get will probably not all agree.

But every boy will admit that there is one and only one *right* answer. Similarly, we believe that in every actual situation, only one action is possible which is right; and that in precisely similar situations precisely similar actions will always be right.

(3) True moral judgments are *impartial*. Perfect impartiality is one of the rarest things in the world. If we consider only our own feelings and emotions, our own likes and dislikes, we cannot be impartial. Our feelings constantly lead us to be partial in our judgments and in our actions. Our feelings naturally tend to make us judge ourselves more leniently than we judge others. Actions which we condemn in strangers we condone in our friends. The teacher finds that his personal affection or dislike for a pupil makes it difficult to treat him impartially. Yet he recognises that he *ought* to be impartial. The moral standard stands above his feelings. Moral judgment should always seek to be impartial and disinterested. It can be so, only when it is definitely rational. Only when we deliberately reflect can we counteract the perverting influences of feeling.

(4) Finally, moral judgments must be *authoritative*. They should be made by the self as a whole, and have behind them not only the weight of the whole self, but also the authority of Reason. As we have seen, conscience is simply the self regarded as passing moral judgments, and conscience has absolute authority because it is the rational self. The free and rational self is, in the fullest sense, the author of its actions and its judgments. But its judgments are not completely authoritative, unless they are in accordance with the authority of Reason.

On all these grounds we conclude that moral judgment is essentially rational judgment. If a moral judgment is to satisfy the demands of objectivity, universality, impartiality, and authoritativeness, it must be based on reason. We have traced the evolution of moral judgment from its earliest beginnings in the life of the child, and have found that unless the judgment be based on reason it cannot be valid. This is an important conclusion.

For further reading : H. Rashdall : *Theory of Good and Evil*, vol. i. ch. vi. ; J. M. Baldwin : *Social and Ethical Interpretations*, ch. iii. and vi. ; G. E. Moore : *Ethics*, ch. iii. and iv.

CHAPTER X.

THE MOTIVES AND SANCTIONS OF CONDUCT

§ 1. Preliminary Remarks. Moral judgment, if it is to be valid, must, we have seen, be based on reason. Now, this important conclusion leads us on immediately to ask other questions. Merely to know that sound moral judgment must be rational does not, after all, take us very far. We need to know, in addition, what exactly are the rational principles that we apply in moral judgment. Accordingly, in this chapter we consider two very important questions which are frequently asked in ordinary life, and to which it is difficult, without some reflection, to give a satisfactory answer. It is often asked, "What makes an action right?" "Is it right because its motive is good or because its consequences are good?" Less frequently the even more fundamental question is asked, "Why should I be good?" "What is the use of living a good life?" In attempting to answer the former question, we must investigate the precise meaning and relation of "motive" and "consequence"; and the answer to the latter will involve a discussion of the "sanctions" of conduct.

140 AN INTRODUCTION TO ETHICS

§ 2. **Analysis of a Typical Moral Action.** In order to make clear the relation between motive and consequence, let us examine a typical moral action. A certain school-girl is very jealous of a rival, and in an important examination cheats in order to obtain a coveted scholarship. Incidentally the winner of the scholarship is always required to recite a Latin ode. The girl's dishonesty is discovered, and she is expelled. If we analyse this action, we may distinguish several factors. (*a*) The girl has a certain *feeling* towards her rival : she is jealous of her. (*b*) She has a certain *aim* in cheating : she wants to secure the scholarship, and she acts in order to attain this end. (*c*) She foresees that the realisation of this end involves as an accompaniment or accessory the recitation of the Latin ode. She does not act as she does in order to recite the ode. She does not want to do that. But she recognises that she cannot have the scholarship without this accessory. (*d*) The actual result of her action is her expulsion from school.

So far, we have analysed the action completely without mentioning the words motive, intention, and consequence. But we must now ask, with reference to this concrete moral action, what these important ethical terms mean. The girl's *motive* for doing the action included her feeling of jealousy, and also the end which she wished to attain. Her *intention* in doing the action included the end which she purposed and the accompaniment which she foresaw. The total *consequence* of the action, as foreseen by her, was identical with the intention. The actual consequence, however, *i.e.* her expulsion from school, was quite different. We may express the results of this investigation in the form of equations.

$$M = F + E,$$
$$I = E + A,$$
$$C = E + A = I,$$
$$C_1 = ? \quad (C_1 = C) \text{ or } (C_1 \neq C).$$

These equations [1] are true of every action. Take, for instance, the action of General Joffre in commanding a general resumption of the offensive on the Marne on September 6th, 1914. His motive in doing this included the aim of driving back the Germans, and also his own complex feeling of love of his country $(M = E + F)$. His intention included this aim, and also the accompaniment of it, *e.g.* the deaths of thousands of his own men. He did not act as he did in order that they might be killed. But he foresaw that their deaths were a necessary accompaniment of the end with a view to which he acted $(I = E + A)$. The total consequences of his action, as he purposed them, were identical with his intention $(C = E + A = I)$. And the actual consequences, which, when he gave the order, were unknown to him $(C_1 = ?)$, coincided to a considerable extent with the purposed consequences $(C_1 = C)$.

§ 3. **Is Motive or Consequence the Test of Right and Wrong?** If we bear carefully in mind the meanings we have assigned to motive and consequence, it will

---

[1] M stands for *motive*, F for *feeling*, E for *end*, A for *accessory*, I for *intention*, C for *consequences* (foreseen, purposed, or intended), and C_1 for *actual consequences*. To the person who is performing a particular action, the actual consequences are unknown $(C_1 = ?)$. They *may* be the consequences which he intended. In that case $C_1 = C$. But they may be quite different. In that case $C_1 \neq C$.

readily be seen that there can be only one answer to this question. The rightness of an action depends upon the motive, the total motive, with which it is performed.

The controversy which has raged between those who believe that motive is the criterion, and those who are convinced that the only objective test is consequence, is very largely due to a failure to take the terms motive and consequence in the strict sense. It has sometimes been argued, for instance, that motive means (1) merely the feeling with which the action is performed, or (2) merely the end or aim which is purposed. Now, if motive be taken in either of these partial senses, it is clear that the rightness of an action cannot depend on the motive. This may be shown in detail in each of the two cases.

(1) If motive be taken in the former sense, it means the actual feeling, emotion, or desire, which impels the action or accompanies it during its performance. A man may be moved by compassion for a beggar, and this emotion may impel the action of giving him a coin. Or he may be carried away by intense anger, and be immediately impelled to action. But in every case in which a man acts in obedience solely to the impulsion of a feeling, his action is not really a completely moral action. Such actions are literally impulsive, for they have not been deliberated on. They are not purposeful: they have no definite aim in view.

If we take deliberate and purposeful actions such as Joffre's and the deceitful girl's, in which, as we have seen, there is both a definite end and a system of feelings, can we say that the rightness of the action depends solely on the feelings ? Was Joffre's action right merely because he loved his country ? Was the girl's deception wrong, simply because she felt jealous of her rival ? It would be absurd to believe that. The rightness and wrongness of actions depends not on the feeling alone, but on the feeling *plus* the end that is purposed. And both of these are included in the motive.

(2) It follows that it is just as erroneous to take motive to include only the end that is purposed. If motive be understood only in that sense, then it must be maintained that the rightness and wrongness of actions have nothing to do with the emotional disposition of the person who performs them. But that is simply not true. If a man gives £50,000 to build an hospital, his act is not morally right unless he feels sympathy with the people whose sufferings his money is destined to alleviate. Here again we see that an action is morally right only if the motive is complete, *i.e.* comprehends both the end purposed and the emotions felt.

Again, those who maintain that consequences constitute the criterion of the rightness or wrongness of actions often do not make clear what precisely they mean by consequences. " Consequences," as we have seen, may mean either (1) the intention, *i.e.* the total results of the action as purposed and foreseen, or (2) the actual results of the action when it has been performed.

Now, in neither of these senses do the consequences of an action supply an adequate test of the rightness or wrongness of that action. With regard to the former case, in which " consequences " is taken to mean " intended consequences," it will be enough to point out that it shares the defect which we have just found to be inherent in the view that the criterion is motive regarded solely as end. It does not take into account the feeling-disposition of the agent. And that is a fatal shortcoming.

In the latter sense, where " consequences " means " actual consequences," the theory is, of course, exposed to precisely the same criticism. And it has, in addition, other defects of its own. It is monstrous to make the rightness of an action depend on the actual consequences, for these are often not in the power of the agent. When we judge that an action is right or wrong, we are always passing a judgment at the same time on the character of the agent, whose action it is. And it is absurd to base our judgment on him on consequences over which he had no control. Of course, he *may* be responsible for the consequences. The evil consequences of his action may be due to his own lack of foresight and reflection. But it very frequently happens that, through no fault of his own, the actual consequences of his action are very different from those which he purposed.[1]

---

[1] Other defects in this theory might be mentioned. It is often impossible to compute the consequences of an action, even after it has been done. They are often strictly incalculable, for they are capable of influencing generations yet unborn. Who could measure the total consequences of Luther's action, in burning the Pope's Bull, or the Kaiser's (if the responsibility be his) in initiating the European War ? Further, even if this test were valid, it would be of use only in assessing the rightness or wrongness of actions which had already been performed. We cannot pretend to know the results of actions which are merely purposed. Hence such a test as this would be of no use to a man who was in doubt as to which of two alternative courses of action he ought to pursue.

Our conclusion, then, is that the rightness and wrongness of actions depends not on the intended consequences alone, nor on the actual consequences alone, nor on the feelings of the agent alone, but on the total motive, which includes both the feelings of the agent and the end for the sake of which the action is performed. Unless both are good, the action will not be right.

§ 4. **Why should I be Good?** Suppose, in a given situation, it is clear that a given action is right. There is no doubt that this action, and this alone, is right. And suppose I say, "This action is doubtless right. It is the action that a good man would perform. But why should I do it? Why should I be good?" In attempting to answer this question, we must consider what are known as the sanctions of conduct. The word sanction is derived from the Latin word *sanctio*, which means "the act of binding" or "that which serves to bind." The word came to have a specifically legal sense. The sanction of a legal enactment is the penalty which is incurred when the law is broken. A man is "bound over" to keep the peace, and it is stipulated that unless he keeps the peace, he will have to pay the penalty. The fear of punishment is thus, from the legal standpoint, the sanction of his good conduct. Various sanctions may be appealed to as reasons why right actions should be done, and wrong ones avoided, but perhaps the most common is the sanction of punishment. If you do this wrong action, it is said, you will be punished; and if you don't do that right action, you will be punished.

§ 5. **The Sanction of Punishment.** Suppose a

mother sees her young son climb a neighbour's apple-tree, pick an unripe apple, and begin to eat it. She calls him to her and says, "Tommy, it is wrong to pick apples that don't belong to you." If Tommy be in a contentious mood, he may protest, "But why shouldn't I do what's wrong? Why should I be good?" Mother may reply, "Because you will be punished if you do wrong." And if mother is inclined to be expansive, she may describe some of the kinds of punishment that await boys who steal unripe apples. (1) Green apples make your stomach very sore. (2) The policeman will catch you. (3) Mother and father and grannie and cook won't like you. (4) Boys who steal apples may go to the bad place when they die.

These are the four kinds of sanction which Bentham, the founder of the Utilitarian School of Ethics, considered most important in the moral life. By the Utilitarians the sanctions are called (1) the physical sanction, (2) the political sanction, (3) the social sanction, and (4) the religious sanction. These are precisely the sanctions that the mother has used in persuading her boy not to steal apples. A word or two must be said about each of them.

(1) The physical sanctions include the pains of body and mind that follow the disregard of natural laws, *e.g.* the headache which follows an evening's carouse. (2) The political sanction consists of the pains and penalties which are attached to the violation of the legal enactments of the State. The law of the land enjoins certain actions and prohibits others. It prohibits theft, libel, assault and battery, etc. It enjoins the paying of rates and taxes, the

maintenance of children, and so on. To each of these prohibitions and injunctions legal penalties are attached. (3) The social sanction depends on public opinion. If you do certain things, you will be " sent to Coventry," " cut " by your friends, shunned by your " set," become ostracised by society, and " lose caste." These sanctions operate in every grade of society and at every age, and the punishment they inflict is often of the severest kind. (4) The religious sanction comprises the pains of Hell, and the penalties by which some churches maintain discipline.

So far, we have considered the sanctions only as pains and penalties. But the sanctions also offer rewards to those whose conduct conforms to their requirements. The man who does right will be rewarded.

§ 6. **The Sanction of Success.** Under each of the four typical classes of sanction some reward or some kind of success is offered to the man who does right. (1) According to the physical sanction, if you live a temperate life, you will be healthy. You will have the physical reward of your moral goodness. Health is almost essential to success. Hence, if you would be successful, live a good life. (2) If you conform to the laws of the land, says the political sanction, they will forward your success. The laws prevent your clerks embezzling your money, they protect the ships in which your merchandise is carried, and they preserve the integrity of your country. Therefore obey the laws, for by so doing you strengthen them and directly contribute to your own success. (3) The social sanction has even more obvious advantages to offer. If you are good, you will be well thought of by society. You will gain reputation, society will give you a "good character," and conformity to social convention will go far to advance your success. (4) Lastly, the religious sanction holds out, as an incentive to virtue, the reward of Heaven, and the prospect of eternal bliss.

The sanction of success is, in one respect, obviously higher than the sanction of punishment. The former encourages action, whereas the latter sets a premium on inaction. The ambition to attain success is a positive thing, whereas the anxiety to avoid punishment is negative. And, as we have seen, the positive life is better than the negative.

§ 7. **Criticism of the Sanctions.** But whether the sanctions be regarded from the positive or negative point of view, they are equally open to fatal criticism. (1) The sanctions are external to conduct. They import their reasons from outside, from facts which are foreign to conduct. If a man does an action, merely because some external sanction advises it, his action is not really moral at all. It has no moral motive. The reasons given by the sanctions why certain actions should be done and others avoided are not really moral at all. Now the justification of a moral act must always itself be moral. It will not do to attempt to justify a moral action by referring to some physical pain or pleasure, that will attend its avoidance or performance. Nor can moral actions be sanctioned by pointing to the legal, social, and religious consequences of them. These associations and consequences are all non-moral; they are all external to the action. A man who abstains from an evil action only because he fears the physical consequences of it, or the legal penalties which it involves, or the social unpopularity which it will reflect upon him, or the pains which religion attaches to it, is not really good. He has abstained from the wrong act, not because it is wrong, not because his character is good and abhors it, but solely because he fears the consequences of the action.

(2) Actions which are done in obedience to the external sanctions of morality, and in accordance with the rules which they imply, may be outwardly indistinguishable from right actions, but they are not right. If a suburban lady gives half-a-crown to a charitable institution simply because all the other ladies in the Terrace do so, she is acting in obedience to the external social sanction, and her action has no moral worth. Her action would be right only if the motive were good, *i.e.* only if she felt sympathy with the institution, and gave her half-crown in order that it might contribute to the realisation of that aim. Actions are not right because they conform to some moral rule. They are right only if they are the expressions of a good character and are prompted by good motives.

The sanctions of morality, as we have seen, are attempts to answer the question, "Why should I be good?" And we have also seen that no sanction can give a satisfactory answer to this question. The only sound answer to the question, "Why should I be good?" is, "Because it is good to be good." Good conduct is its own sufficient justification. Morality contains in itself its own sanctions. To the man of good character, his own approval is the highest reward, and his own remorse the severest punishment. Goodness is an intrinsic thing, which depends on no external sanctions and extraneous associations.

§ 8. **The Educational Value of External Sanctions.** Yet these sanctions have a certain educational value. The child cannot understand the absoluteness of morality. "Be good simply because it is good" seems to him an intolerably vague precept. If he asks, "Why should I do this particular right action?" it conveys no information to him to be told, "Because it is right." He wants a definite and particular answer to a particular and definite question. It is just here that the sanctions have value.

(1) The sanctions give readily intelligible reasons for conduct. These reasons are definite and limited. If we revert to the case of the boy and the apples, it is clear that he will have no difficulty in understanding the nature of the sanctions to which his mother appeals. He knows what it is to have a sore stomach. He knows what a policeman is. He knows what it is to be regarded by the whole household as a "naughty boy." And he has been impressed with the awfulness of the "bad place." External sanctions are educationally valuable because they are easily understood, and make an immediate impression on the mind.

(2) External sanctions have great persuasive value. When the object is simply to get a child to do an action, they are often indispensable. The child may be very unwilling to perform an action which seems disagreeable to it. "Do this because it is

MOTIVES AND SANCTIONS OF CONDUCT 151

right" will make no impression on it. But "If you do this, you will get a cake," or "If you don't do this, you will get a whipping," will quickly lead it to change its attitude, and do the disagreeable thing. If external sanctions be used in a prudent way to persuade children to courses of action for which at first they have no natural inclination, they may prove a very valuable educational instrument.

(3) Their value depends on the fact that it is important that children should learn to act rightly, or as a good person would act, even before they can be expected to know why they act rightly. The average man acts rightly all his life without reflecting why he does so. And though moral theory is important, moral practice is still more important. As we saw in an earlier chapter, we form good habits only by repeatedly doing right actions. Hence it is exceedingly important that the child should, as soon as possible, be encouraged to do habitually the right actions. In order to attain this result, there is no reason why the external sanctions should not be wisely and prudently used.

(4) But we must insist that these external sanctions should be employed only as a propaedeutic. They are a second-best, and should be used only as stepping stones over which the child may pass to a higher conception of morality. They may be used as a means to persuade the child to do the good and avoid the evil; but the child should never be led to believe that they supply the ultimate reasons why he should be good and do the right. It is impossible to give any *particular* reasons for doing right and being good that will be absolutely true, not because

there are no reasons for being good, but because there is every possible reason.

For further reading: (for §§ 1-3) J. S. Mackenzie: *Manual*, bk. i. ch. ii.; J. H. Muirhead: *Elements*, §§ 21-25; J. Dewey and J. H. Tufts: *Ethics*, pp. 241-257; (for §§ 4-8) J. S. Mackenzie: *Manual*, bk. ii. ch. vi.; Leslie Stephen: *Science of Ethics*, pp. 396-404; J. M. Baldwin: *Social and Ethical Interpretations*, ch. ix. and x.

CHAPTER XI.

THE PLACE OF DUTY IN THE MORAL LIFE.

§ 1. **Moral Obligation**. So far we have been considering conduct from the point of view of the rightness and wrongness of the actions in which it consists. We examined the various sanctions of conduct, and concluded that while these sanctions are of educational value in persuading children to do the right, they are not to be regarded as reasons why the good should be done. There is no reason why we should do the right except simply that it is right. What is right is what I have morally *got* to do. It is my duty to do the right. If I am morally healthy, the right action presents itself to me as the action that I am morally bound to do. It is my "bounden duty."

This consciousness of moral obligation is possible only to a growing self. It is possible only to a self that is aware of its own imperfection, and also of an ideal perfection which it has not yet attained. The sense of moral obligation implies that the self is aware that it ought to perform a certain action. Now, if the self is morally healthy, as soon as it perceives what it ought to do, it will do it. If it is morally healthy, it will regard what it ought to do as the only conceivable course of action for it. But if the self be weak, it may do what it ought not to do, though it realises all the time what it ought to do. Now, whether it actually does what it ought to do, or what it ought not to do, it is equally conscious of moral obligation. It feels that a duty is laid upon it. When it does what it ought to do, it is conscious that it has done its duty : when it does what it ought not to do, it is conscious that it has not done its duty. In both cases alike, the consciousness of duty, of moral obligation, is involved.

§ 2. **Why is it Hard to do our Duty?** Some people find it easy to do their duty. But for the average man it is exceedingly hard. To do our duty involves a moral struggle. The reason for this is that our duty very often conflicts with our inclinations. It is contrary to our desires. It is not in the line of our interests. Duty makes certain requirements to which we have a natural aversion. Duty seems to have an uncanny way of running counter to our wants and preferences.

The child early learns this characteristic of duty. Just when it is most interested in its mud-pies, Duty calls it to be tidied, to be taken to the drawing-room, to be displayed to people in whom it takes no interest whatever. Just when its bricks are rising into the most enchanting castle, Duty summons it to bed. And so on indefinitely. The average child would probably define duty as " what you don't want to do."

The associations which duty thus early acquires often continue to cling to it. There seems to be a natural warfare between duty and our desires and

THE PLACE OF DUTY

inclinations. Now, as we recognised in a previous chapter, the inclinations and desires are natural to man. Without them human life would not be possible. Even if we would, we could not destroy them all. But the progress of the moral life consists in controlling and organising them. Every time a desire is restrained there is a contest for supremacy between inclination and duty. We want to satisfy the desire, but we know that it is our duty to repress it. Because our impulses are so spontaneous, our appetites so insistent, and our desires so importunate, duty must again and again come into conflict with them. Thus we come to regard the law of duty as set over against our lawless and unruly impulses and desires.

But we must not make the mistake of thinking that duty never conflicts with anything but impulse and passion. It may be our duty to gratify a natural appetite or impulse against a formed and consistent habit of life. The scientist may become so engrossed in his experiments that he may forget for a day at a time the need of satisfying the natural appetite of hunger. Here it is his duty to leave his laboratory for a few minutes to satisfy his bodily needs. The student may be so anxious about his work that he neglects natural desires for relaxation. In such a case it is his duty to play tennis of an evening for the sake of his health. Again, it may be a businessman's duty to obey an impulse of pity, in opposition to his formed habit of life, which tells him that it is "unbusinesslike." In all these cases, though duty lies on the side of appetite and impulse and instinct, it is always in conflict with the dominant interest.

The scientist's interest is concentrated on his experiment, and that is why he finds it hard to do his duty by interrupting it and satisfying his hunger. The student's interest is engrossed in his studies, and the business-man's interest is wholly engaged by his business. It is difficult for them to do their duty in obeying natural impulses, because these run counter to their dominant interests.

We may state, then, the general truth that it is hard for us to do our duty, because our duty so often conflicts with our dominant interests. The stress and strain of the moral life arise from the conflict of duty and interest. But it is not necessary that duty and interest should always be opposed. Duty and interest may be in perfect accord. And one of the great tasks of the moral teacher, as we shall see more fully later on, is to educate men so that their interests may be in harmony with their duty.

§ 3. **Rules of Duty.** We have seen that even when we clearly recognise what our duty is, it may be hard to do it. But it is often equally difficult to know what our duty is. What is my duty? Can ethics give any answer to that question? Can ethics give any list of rules, by following which we may be sure always to know what our duty is? In other departments of knowledge and behaviour such systems of rules do exist. The child is early given a set of rules with regard to good manners. In most of the arts there are bodies of rules, which are always or generally true, and by acting in accordance with which the student is likely to turn out good work. Is there anything corresponding to this in ethics? Are there definite rules of conduct, obedience to which

THE PLACE OF DUTY

will guarantee right action ? Now, there certainly are vast numbers of moral rules, in which the child is often instructed with much earnestness and persistence. "Under all variety of circumstances, in season and often out of season, we are fed on a diet of line upon line and precept upon precept. Children find precepts on the walls of their nurseries, and boys and girls in the headings of their copy-books. When the country girl leaves her home, it is with a precept her mother bids her farewell ; and it is with a precept that the father sends out his boy to make his way in the world." [1]

There is no doubt that the moral experience of mankind is to a large extent embodied in these precepts, whether they be commonplaces of moralists, lines from the poets, proverbs of the people, or commandments of God. And it is natural that these moral rules should have an influence in shaping the lives of men and women.

(1) Yet the ethical value of such moral rules is very limited. If, in a concrete situation, we merely act according to a moral rule, in accordance with a formula which we have learnt by rote, our action really has no moral value. This follows from all that was said in the previous chapter. If a moral action is simply in accordance with a moral rule, simply in blind conformity to it, then the action is not really a moral action. It has no motive. If I respect my parents simply because the fifth commandment enjoins that duty, then my action has strictly no moral value.

(2) Precepts of all kinds are often mere counsels

[1] MacCunn : *The Making of Character*, p. 179.

of prudence. The duties they advise are those which are calculated to make a man "Healthy, wealthy, and wise." Now, health, wealth, and wisdom are all desirable ; but they do not constitute the moral end. Duty looks to a far higher ideal than that.

And if we pay too much attention to precepts and proverbs, we are apt to discover that it is perilously easy to find precepts to justify any action that is most convenient and profitable to ourselves. It is wonderful how readily we can find particular precepts to support what we want to do, even if we know that what we want to do is really wrong.

(3) But even if we are sincere in seeking the help of precepts, even if we apply to them not to give us good reasons for doing what is wrong, but to guide us in moral perplexities to do what is right, we discover that they are of very little practical assistance. If we think of one precept which advises one course of action, we are pretty sure to remember another which counsels precisely the opposite. It is notorious that precepts, especially those that have become proverbial, contradict one another. "We have a dozen to tell us that honesty is the best policy ; a dozen more to say that the children of this world are wiser than the children of light. Some to declare that like draws to like, and others that extremes meet ; a host to persuade us that to hesitate is to be lost, and we are almost persuaded—till we remember that second thoughts are best. As many to decide that it is never too late to mend ; and as many more to pronounce that as the tree falls so it must lie." [1]

[1] MacCunn : *The Making of Character*, p. 181.

THE PLACE OF DUTY

Even when rules of conduct have been organised into a system and become a definite moral code, it may be impossible to apply them in concrete moral situations. If we attempt to apply the Ten Commandments, we soon find that it may be impossible to observe one commandment without breaking another. Conflicts may take place between two commandments. In all such cases of conflict, we are bound to ask, Which law has superior authority ? Which is the greatest commandment ? Which is the supreme principle of duty ?

A comprehensive principle of duty was suggested by Kant and formulated thus : " Act only on that maxim which thou canst at the same time will to become a universal law." Unless I am ready to will that the act which I am going to perform should become a universal law, and be performed by all other human beings, my act is not right. Telling the truth is right, because I can will that everybody should always tell the truth. Committing suicide is wrong, because if I willed that suicide should become universal, the whole human race would disappear. And I cannot will that. Giving way to utter idleness is wrong, for I cannot will that all men should live in idleness and fail to develop their faculties.

Kant illustrates the working of the principle in detail. "A man finds himself forced by necessity to borrow money. He knows that he will not be able to repay it, but sees also that nothing will be lent to him, unless he promises stoutly to repay it in a definite time. He desires to make this promise, but he has still so much conscience as to ask himself : Is it not unlawful and inconsistent with duty to get out of a difficulty in this way ? Suppose, however, that he resolves to do so, then the maxim of his action would be expressed thus : When I think myself in want of money, I will borrow money, and promise to repay it, although I know that I never can do so. Now this principle of self-love or of one's own advantage may perhaps be consistent with my whole future welfare ; but the question now is, Is it right ? I change then the suggestion of self-love into a universal law, and state the question thus : How would it be if my maxim were a universal law ? Then I see at once that it could never hold as a universal law of nature, but would necessarily contradict itself. For, supposing it to be a universal law that everyone when he thinks himself in a difficulty should be able to promise whatever he pleases, with the purpose of not keeping his promise, the promise itself would become impossible, as well as the end that one might have in view in it, since no one would consider that anything was promised to him, but would ridicule all such statements as vain pretences." [1]

A moral principle such as this may be of considerable value in helping us to see that certain actions really are wrong. Many people who would scorn to steal will cheerfully evade the income-tax. They might be surprised if such evasion were named theft. But it certainly is theft, for I am really stealing from the State the sum that I ought to have paid, and indirectly I am taking it from the pockets of each and all of my neighbours. The wrongness of the evasion becomes very evident, if an attempt is

[1] *The Metaphysic of Morals* (Abbott's translation), p. 40.

THE PLACE OF DUTY

made to universalise it. Can I will that everybody shall evade his income-tax? I cannot, and therefore see clearly that the action is wrong.

But even such a comprehensive principle as this is inadequate to the complexity of life. For it altogether excludes exceptions. And morality is really made up of exceptional cases, in the sense that the moral life consists of particular actions, and particular actions are always performed in particular circumstances. An action that may be right under certain conditions may be quite wrong in other circumstances. There is no moral rule, however comprehensive, which may not have to be broken under certain circumstances. It is a fundamental moral principle that murder is a sin. But who would say that the man who in the Indian Mutiny killed his wife to prevent her falling into the hands of the mutinous sepoys did wrong? Again, it is a sin to tell a lie. But under certain circumstances, it may be quite right to speak falsely with the intention of deceiving. In war it is right for a captured soldier to give false information to his captors. Perhaps ordinary morality may exclaim, "Oh, but I don't call that a lie." It *is* a lie. But the duty always to tell the truth has been overborne by a higher duty.

Are we then to conclude that moral rules are simply made to be broken? Hardly so. Moral rules, as we have seen, do have a certain value. They do hold true on the whole. They are like rules in medicine, which are true in most cases, and are helpful in dealing with most instances of the diseases to which they apply. But they are always liable to exception. Peculiar cases may occur in which they do not apply. The good doctor recognises that his rules are true only on the whole, and that he must not follow them blindly. He must use his insight to decide when they are inapplicable. It is very similar with ethics. The good man will bear in mind the moral rules which he has been taught, the proverbs and commandments which have helped to shape his life, but he will remember that they are always liable to exception, and he will use his moral insight to decide when and where they apply. But while we recognise that all moral rules are liable to exception, it is worth noticing the *kind* of exception of which they admit. A law of duty must never be broken to satisfy a whim or desire. Never break a law of duty simply to please yourself. One moral rule may be broken only for the sake of a higher moral rule. A duty may be ignored or postponed only for the sake of an over-ruling duty.

§ 4. **The Authority of Duty.** The conception of duty always involves the consciousness of the existence of some authority with which the duty is invested and by which it is commanded. We commonly speak of duties being "laid upon us," of obligations "imposed upon us"; and these phrases indicate that there is some authority which imposes the duty. What is the authority?

The authority of the moral law is only gradually apprehended. In the mind of the child the moral law seems to be embodied in the will of its mother and father. For the child their commands constitute the moral law: their commands have absolute authority. But his parents may be the first to point out to him that their commands are not simply *theirs*. They rest on some more ultimate authority.

They may suggest that the ultimate moral authority is the law of the land. What the law of the land commands is right, and what it forbids is wrong. But this conception of the authority of the moral law is defective; and in two ways. In the first place, the law of the land is not so comprehensive as the moral law. The law of the land places no restriction upon a host of actions which the moral law declares to be wrong. The moral law states that they are wrong, whether they are punishable under the law of the land or not. Further, it is simply not true that the authority of the moral law or duty depends on the law of the land. It is the other way about. The law of the land depends for its authority on the moral law. An action is not wrong because the law of the land says it is wrong. The law of the land says it is wrong because it *is* wrong, and unless the act is wrong in itself, the law of the land cannot make it so. There is an authority superior to the law of the land.

Does this authority reside in the will of God ? Such a code of moral law as the Ten Commandments derives its authority from the will of Jehovah. The moral laws of the Mohammedans are dependent for their authority on the will of Allah as revealed in the Koran. But the moral consciousness soon begins to perceive defects in this formulation of the authority of the moral law. The will of God is revealed in various Holy Books, the Bible, the Koran, and so on. Now the moral laws enshrined in these revelations of God's will are not consistent. The different statements of the moral law conflict. For instance, the Bible says that polygamy is wrong, whereas the Koran says that it is right. The question therefore arises, Which statement is true ? Which is the supreme authority ? The Christian will say the authority of the Bible, and the Mohammedan the authority of the Koran ; and it will be impossible to reach any agreement. But we have already seen that the authority of the moral law must be absolute, and its commands must be universally binding. The law of God is authoritative only to the man who believes in God. But the moral law of duty must carry a universal obligation.

And there is a further defect which is characteristic of all these views of the nature of moral authority. The authority to which they appeal is always external. It is always imposed from outside. The authority of parents, the authority of the law of the land, and the authority of God are all alike in this, that the seat of the authority is external to the agent himself. Now a duty is a moral duty only when it is self-imposed. A duty is my duty only when I recognise that, whatever external sanctions it may possess, it is laid upon me by myself. My conscience acknowledges that it is a duty for me, and my will imposes it upon me as a line of action that ought to be carried out. The duty is an obligation laid upon the self by the self.

§ 5. **Duty and the Self.** This aspect of duty is usually expressed by ethical writers in the statement that in morality the will should be autonomous. The will should not be at the mercy of any authority outside it and foreign to its nature. The will must be its own master, and when it obeys a paramount authority it does so because it acknowledges that the authority has a right to command. It recognises the authority as cognate to itself, and itself wills the action that authority commands. Its obedience to authority is not externally compelled : it is freely willed. The self must itself will to perform its duties.

This does not mean that the self is at liberty to regard as its duty any line of action it pleases to choose. In general, it is a man's duty to conform to the obligations which established authority imposes. But he should learn to appreciate *why* they are duties. Obedience to authority rests on the assumption that the moral experience of generations of men, which has been embodied in the existing moral authority, is likely to contain much that is true and good. The individual's moral judgments are very apt to be warped by passions and emotions ; and he should make very sure of himself before opposing established moral authority. In particular, Green has suggested the useful practical maxim, " While a man may not go far wrong in imposing on himself some new restraint which is not generally recognised by his contemporaries, he ought to hesitate very much longer before he allows himself any indulgence which the accepted morality condemns."

There are certain duties which are expected of every member of the community. It is a duty for every man to tell the truth, to be honest, to pay his debts, to earn his living, and so on. But over and above these general duties, which are common to all members of the community, and are imposed by the general moral authority of the community as a whole, there is a host of special duties which are obligatory on a man in virtue of the particular position he occupies in the community. Every citizen has some position in the State, and enters into some relationships with his fellow-men. These positions and relationships not only enrich him with certain privileges and invest him with certain rights, but they also make certain demands on him and imply certain duties. Thus, in a man's domestic relationships, as a son or brother or husband or father, he finds that certain duties pertain to him. These duties vary according to the relationship in which he stands. The duties of the son are not those of the father. Again, the particular calling which a man adopts carries with it a system of particular duties which are obligatory upon him in virtue of his calling. These duties vary according as he is a doctor, clergyman, lawyer, artisan, labourer or soldier. But in addition to these particular groups of duties, each man has duties which are peculiar to him, and in which no one else can share. These duties he can recognise as duties only by a kind of moral insight. No moral rules will help him here. In order to realise his duties he must cultivate the duteous spirit, the attitude of conscientiousness.

For further reading: J. H. Muirhead: *Elements*, bk. iv. ch. i.; J. S. Mackenzie: *Manual*, bk. ii. ch. iii., bk. iii. ch. iii.; Kant: *Metaphysic of Morals*, first section. T. H. Green: *Prolegomena to Ethics*, §§ 206-217.

CHAPTER XII.

THE PLACE OF PLEASURE IN THE MORAL LIFE.

§ 1. **Pleasure and Life.** In every life pleasure plays a part of great importance. Whether a man be a saint or a sinner, a roué or an ascetic, a "good fellow" or a hermit, he cannot get away from pleasure. He may wallow in the enjoyment of pleasures, or spurn them with a noble contempt, but in both cases pleasure is a factor to be reckoned with. All or nearly all our conduct is pervaded by pleasurable or painful feeling. All our experience is accompanied by what the psychologist terms an affective tone, or a hedonic tone, which may either be agreeable or disagreeable. The affective tone of some of our perceptions and actions may be so vague as to be apparently non-existent. When we are doing some very simple and habitual action, such as dressing or sharpening a pencil, the hedonic tone of the action may not be present in our consciousness at all. With reference to pleasure and pain the action is simply neutral. But even such simple actions tend to have a definite affective tone. If the morning be cold, dressing is felt to be disagreeable, and when one is using a very sharp knife the act of sharpening the pencil may be distinctly pleasant.

We may affirm, then, that practically all our experience has an affective tone. It is either pleasant or unpleasant, either agreeable or disagreeable.

It is obviously important to consider what attitude we ought to adopt towards pleasure. Is pleasure good or evil ? Ought we to seek pleasure or shun it ? No question, perhaps, in the whole field of ethics has been discussed with such persistence ; and on no question has there been more strongly marked diversity of opinion.

§ 2. **Hedonism.** From the dawn of ethical speculation there have been thinkers who have maintained that the great aim of life is the attainment of pleasure. These thinkers are called Hedonists. (The name is derived from the Greek word for pleasure.) One of the earliest Hedonists was Aristippus, who was born about 435 B.C. He held that the great aim of life is to enjoy the pleasures of the moment. Man should not " look before and after " ; he should think only of the moment, and throw all his energies into the enjoyment of each pleasure as it comes. The hot blood of Africa ran in Aristippus's veins, and he and his followers put their theory into practice by indulging in all sorts of pleasures indiscriminately.

This crude theory was polished and elevated by Epicurus (341-270 B.C.), who saw that an existence made up simply of pleasurable moments could not be the best life for man. Such a life might be adequate for animals. But it is man's nature to be able to reflect and anticipate ; man's life is not merely a series of disconnected moments, it is a relatively persistent and consistent whole. Therefore, Epicurus says, man should not desire simply the pleasures of the moment. He should aim at pleasures that endure, lasting satisfactions, permanent states of agreeable feeling. Hence the Epicureans maintain that calm satisfaction is preferable to violent excitement. The aim of life is to attain a pleasurable tranquillity, an equable contentment with whatever gifts fortune may deign to bestow. The Epicureans also practised what they preached, and in their quiet garden at Athens they enjoyed a simple life of pleasant contentment and peaceful calm.

§ 3. **Utilitarianism.** Hedonism was more systematically formulated by Bentham (1748-1832) and John Stuart Mill (1806-1873), and came to be called Utilitarianism. Utilitarianism is thus a developed Hedonism. All Utilitarians may be called Hedonists, but all Hedonists are not Utilitarians. Utilitarianism is a kind of Hedonism. Utilitarianism differs in two respects from the Hedonism of the Epicureans.

(1) It is not selfish. It does not bid a man take into account only his own pleasures. It commands him to have regard to the general happiness of the community as a whole. The Epicurean did not explicitly consider the pleasure of others. Each man was concerned only with himself and took an interest only in his own pleasures; and in so far as he took account of the pleasure of other persons, *e.g.* his friends, it was because his own pleasure lay in consulting their interests and desires. Utilitarianism, on the contrary, insists that the moral end is " not the agent's own greatest happiness, but the greatest amount of happiness altogether." Each person should be just as eager that others should attain

pleasure as that he should. "As between his own happiness and that of others, Utilitarianism requires him to be as strictly impartial as a disinterested and benevolent spectator." The Utilitarians state, as a fundamental formula, "Each to count for one, and no one for more than one." Utilitarianism demands perfect impartiality in conduct : we must treat each man as one whose claim to enjoy pleasure is equal to our own ; and we must aim at the greatest possible amount of pleasure for all human beings or for all sentient creatures.

(2) Utilitarianism also differs from earlier types of Hedonism by introducing a distinction of quality between pleasures. Before J. S. Mill no Hedonist admitted that pleasures can differ in quality. The only differences between pleasures, it was believed, were quantitative. If the amount of pleasure was the same, the value of it was the same. The only way one pleasure could be superior to another was that there should be more of it. The Epicureans had, indeed, distinguished pleasures of the mind from pleasures of the body ; but not because the one is better than the other. Rather, pleasures of the mind, being finer and calmer, are more lasting than those of the body, and less likely to lead to painful consequences. Hence they are greater in amount.

But Mill protested that if we are to be true to the facts of life, we must recognise that pleasures differ in quality as well as in quantity. " It would be absurd," says Mill, " that while, in estimating all other things, quality is considered as well as quantity, the estimation of pleasure should be supposed to depend on quantity alone." Thus, instead of saying,

PLEASURE IN THE MORAL LIFE 171

" Seek the *most* pleasure possible," Mill would say, " Seek the *best* pleasure possible." Now the quality of pleasure can be judged only by those who have had the widest and wisest experience of it. Connoisseurs in pleasure will balance pleasures against one another, and " if one of the two is, by those who are competently acquainted with both, placed so far above the other that they prefer it, even though knowing it to be attended with a greater amount of discontent, and would not resign it for any amount of other pleasure which their nature is capable of, we are justified in ascribing to the preferred enjoyment a superiority in quality, so far outweighing it as to render it, in comparison, of small account."

Now, this distinction which Mill introduced puts a higher complexion on Hedonism. " Seek the best pleasure possible " is clearly a more elevating precept than " Seek the most pleasure possible." But the two main criticisms to which all Hedonism is open apply also to the lofty Utilitarianism of Mill. For there are two convictions which are common to all Hedonists, whether Utilitarians or not. These are (1) that pleasure is the only object of desire, and (2) that pleasure is the standard of moral action and moral judgment. Pleasure for Hedonism is both the moral end and the moral standard. These points are very important, and the Hedonist view must be examined with some care.

§ 4. **Is Pleasure the Moral Standard?** Utilitarianism maintains that pleasure is the only moral standard. If I want to know, in given circumstances, whether an act is right or not, I have only to ask myself, Does it (along with its consequences) contain the greatest amount of pleasure possible under the circumstances ? If it does, it is right. If it does not, it is wrong. Now this standard seems at first sight a delightfully simple one to apply. If three courses of action are open to me, one of which contains 2 units of pleasure, another 3, another 4, then the right course of action is that which contains 4 units of pleasure, because $4 > 3$, and $4 > 2$. But if it were possible to combine the first two courses of action, then the combined course is right, because $3 + 2 > 4$. Now, all this sounds very simple. But as soon as we examine the standard a little more closely, we find that it is, in reality, very complicated indeed.

In the first place, how are we to calculate the quantitative value of pleasures ? Suppose at a particular juncture two courses of action are open to us, how are we to decide which is the more pleasant ? Bentham answered that these lines of conduct should be considered in various aspects, with regard to (a) the intensity of the pleasures connected with them, (b) their duration, (c) their certainty, (d) their nearness or remoteness, (e) their fecundity, *i.e.* their tendency to produce other pleasures, (f) their purity, *i.e.* their freedom from pain, and (g) their extent, *i.e.* the number of persons who are affected by them. The values of the pleasures under all these heads should be summed up, and the pains deducted. This process should be repeated for every possible course of action, and that line of conduct which at the end stands highest in value is the right action. But it is very evident that it is impossible to give numerical values to pleasures, and that even if the elaborate process of addition and subtraction could be performed, it would take such a long time that it would generally be impossible to use the standard in dealing with the ordinary difficulties and perplexities of life.[1]

Further, Bentham assumes that we have the power

---

[1] It is interesting to try to apply the standard in a particular case. Suppose at the beginning of March a man is in doubt whether he ought to take a fortnight's holiday alone in the South of France at Easter, or take his family to the Coast for a month in August. He decides to calculate the value of the two courses of action in terms of pleasure according to the Utilitarian method. Call the first course of action X and the second Y. Consider these lines of conduct with reference to the various aspects of pleasure. With regard to (*a*) the intensity of pleasure, X is preferable ; (*b*) with regard to duration, Y is more desirable ; (*c*) X is more certain (he may be dead by the time August comes, and besides, the weather is much more apt to interfere with the enjoyment of the Coast holiday) ; (*d*) in respect to nearness, X is preferable ; (*e*) with regard to fecundity, X is probably preferable (he will have experiences and see things and take photographs on the Mediterranean holiday which will be a constant source of pleasure for months afterwards) ; (*f*) with regard to purity, X is probably again preferable (on the Mediterranean holiday he will be free from the petty irritations and domestic annoyances which are apt to spoil a family holiday for him) ; (*g*) in extent, Y is preferable. Now, if we sum up, without attempting to give numerical values to the preferences we find that on five of the seven counts X is preferable. Thus, it would seem to follow that X is the right course of action. But there is no doubt at all that in most actual cases X would be wrong. It would not be wrong in *all* cases. It depends largely on circumstances. If the father were threatened with consumption, a fortnight's escape from the fog and cold and wet of the North might save his life. Under these circumstances he would act rightly in taking the "selfish" holiday. But in normal circumstances he would be wrong. This illustration shows clearly not only how impossible it is to apply *this* rule to decide concrete cases of rightness and wrongness ; but also that it is unsatisfactory to try to apply mechanically *any* rule to moral actions. The rightness of actions is relative to the self which does them, and is much affected by the circumstances under which they are performed.

of foretelling accurately the nature of the pleasures and pains attaching to the various possible courses of action. But it is a fact of common experience that this is often quite impossible. Our forecasts of future pleasures and pains are often very far wide of the mark. All we can do is to calculate *probable* pleasant and painful consequences. After all our elaborate calculation, our standard does not tell us that such and such an action is right : it merely enables us to say that it is *probably* right.

And another grave objection to pleasure as the standard is that it is open to all the criticisms that we have already brought against the general theory according to which the consequences of an action determine its rightness or wrongness. The view we are considering at present says that an action is right if its total consequences are probably more pleasurable than those of any other possible action under the circumstances. That is, the *consequences* of the action constitute the test of its rightness or wrongness. And this, as we have seen, is not really a moral standard.[1]

§5. **Is Pleasure the Object of Desire ?** Hedonism maintains not only that pleasure is the object of desire, but that it is the *only* object of desire. As a matter of fact, say the Hedonists, all men desire pleasure ; and when they seem to desire other things, they desire them only because they are means to the attainment of pleasure. Ultimately the only thing desired is pleasure.

[1] The criticism in this paragraph, which is really the fundamental one, applies equally to all varieties of Utilitarianism. But the rest of §4, it will have been noticed, has Bentham in view, rather than Mill.

In examining this view, we must first make clear the meaning of pleasure. In ordinary speech we talk of pleasures as if they were definite *things*. We say that a certain man is " a lover of pleasures rather than a lover of God," and we speak of the pleasures of the chase or the pleasures of love or the pleasures of reading. In all these cases we ordinarily mean by pleasures the things in which we find satisfaction. Now, strictly, "pleasure" does not mean the object which gives us satisfaction, but the actual feeling of satisfaction which we have when we attain the object of our desire. Pleasure means agreeable feeling : it is, as we have seen, the affective tone of our experience. Pleasures are nothing but the feelings which accompany the attainment (and in some cases the pursuit) of the object of our desire. What we desire is always a particular object or group of objects, or a particular activity or system of activities. The acquisition of these objects and the performance of these activities is accompanied by the agreeable feeling-tone which we call pleasure.

From this analysis it should be clear that (*a*) while we usually desire objects, the attainment or pursuit of which will be attended by pleasant feeling, (*b*) we may, and often do, desire objects which we recognise will be accompanied by unpleasant feeling, and (*c*) we very rarely make mere pleasant feeling the object of our desire. A word or two must be said on each of these points. It will be convenient to take them in reverse order.

(1) In most of our desires two or more objects are involved. One of these is proximate, the other is remote ; one is narrow and limited, the other is wide

and comprehensive. If I desire to finish writing this chapter, the proximate and narrow object of my desire is simply the cessation of the tiring physical activity of writing. But another object, more comprehensive and remote, is implied. I desire to reach the end of the chapter because it contributes to the completion of the book, and I desire to finish the book in order that it may be in the hands of my students. As we have seen in Chapter IV., our desires can be organised under more and more comprehensive desires, until they become entirely systematised in accordance with a dominant ambition. It is only in very rare cases that pleasant feeling is either a proximate or remote object of desire. No doubt there have been men whose desires have centred in enjoying the greatest variety of pleasurable feelings, and who have organised their whole lives in deference to this aim. And there are men who desire particular objects solely because of the pleasurable feeling which accompanies their attainment. But such men are exceptions. What we desire, in general, is a particular object. We enjoy the feelings which accompany its pursuit and attainment. But what we desire is the object, in so far as it contributes to the realisation of our dominant aims and purposes.

(2) We may desire objects though we are aware that their attainment will be attended with disagreeable feelings. A man desires to be a martyr or to die in his country's cause, though he realises that the torture and death will be accompanied by a very unpleasant affective tone. To take a less extreme case, a man will " scorn delights and live

laborious days," with all their boredom and weariness, in order to advance science or provide for his family. The attainment of these comprehensive ends may be accompanied by pleasurable feeling, but it may not. The man may simply do it because he conceives that it is his duty.

(3) But, in general, the objects that we desire bring with them pleasant feelings. I desire a dish of steak and onions : the eating of it is pleasant. I desire to hear Melba : listening to her singing is pleasant. I desire a game of tennis : the exercise is pleasant. In every case the satisfaction of the desire is attended by pleasant feeling. But that does not mean that we desire the object in order to enjoy the feeling. I may desire the steak and onions because I need nourishment ; I may desire to hear Melba in order to be able to write a descriptive report of her singing ; and I may desire the game of tennis simply for the sake of my health. To think that we desire the object or activity simply for the sake of the pleasure that accompanies it is as absurd as to suppose that, in William James's words, "because no steamer can go to sea without incidentally consuming coal, therefore no steamer can go to sea for any other motive than that of coal-consumption." [1]

§ 6. **Pleasure and the Self.** We conclude, then, that pleasure is neither the supreme moral end nor the standard of judgment. But we admit that pleasure occupies an important place in life. As we have seen, all experience is permeated by pleasure and pain as its affective tone ; and it is eminently

[1] *Principles of Psychology*, ii. p. 558.

desirable that the affective tone of our experience should be as pleasant as possible. But the point to note is that pleasure is morally valuable precisely in proportion as it is not definitely and directly sought for itself. There is no more futile life than that of the " pleasure-seeker." It is a commonplace, confirmed by the experience of ages, that the life of the pleasure-seeker is often the most unhappy of lives. The very term " pleasure-seeker " is suggestive : it suggests that he never attains. And it is the experience of the pleasure-seeker that when he thinks he has attained the pleasures that he covets, they become Dead-Sea fruit. It is natural and necessary that the pleasure-seeker's life should be futile and feckless. His only aim is to secure a changing variety of pleasurable feeling. Now, nothing is so transient as a feeling. One moment it is felt, the next it is gone for ever. The life of pleasure is a life of isolated pleasurable moments. It is a string of beads without the string. Such a life has nothing to give it unity and coherence. Its only aim is aimlessness ; its only purpose confesses a lack of purpose.

Hence the maxim that the only way to get pleasure is to forget it. Pleasant feeling naturally accompanies the healthy exercise of our faculties and the pursuit and attainment of the objects of our desire. The less we think about our pleasures, the more pleasant will our lives become. As Sidgwick has said, " Of our active enjoyments generally . . . it may certainly be said that we cannot attain them, at least in their highest degree, so long as we concentrate our aim on them. . . . Similarly, the pleasures of thought and study can only be enjoyed in the highest degree by those who have an ardour of curiosity, which carries the mind temporarily away from self and its sensations. In all kinds of Art, again, the exercise of the creative faculty is attended by intense and exquisite pleasures ; but in order to get them, one must forget them." [1]

On the whole, this maxim is true ; but we should remember that, while it is never right to seek pleasure solely *for itself*, there *are* times when it may be right to seek pleasure. When I go on holiday, for instance, it is not only right, but it may be a duty, to seek pleasure. In such a case it is right for me to seek pleasure, because enjoyment and relaxation will help to make me more fit to take up the duties of my vocation again after my holiday. The "pleasure-seeker," on the other hand, seeks pleasure *for itself*, and *lives for it* and for nothing else. It is because he lives for the sake of pleasure that he is wrong in seeking it. All pleasure is relative to the self, and derives its moral value from its relation to the self and its dominant purposes.

[1] *Methods of Ethics*, bk. i. ch. iv. p. 47.

For further reading : J. S. Mackenzie : *Manual*, bk. ii. ch. iv. ; J. H. Muirhead : *Elements of Ethics*, bk. iii. ch. i. and iii. ; J. Dewey and J. H. Tufts : *Ethics*, ch. xiv. ; J. Seth : *Study of Ethical Principles*, part i. ch. i. and iii. ; J. Watson : *Hedonistic Theories from Aristippus to Spencer* ; J. S. Mill : *Utilitarianism*, ch. i.-iv.

CHAPTER XIII.

VOCATION.

§ 1. **Pleasure, Duty, and Happiness.** The young child sharply distinguishes between pleasure and duty. What gives it pleasure is the thing it wants to do; while duty always seems to be what it does not want to do. Duty is unpleasant, and pleasure is apt to be undutiful. But the child gradually comes to see that duty is not necessarily externally imposed by some alien power. It realises that it is free, and that it can impose its duties on itself. Similarly, the child begins to recognise that stolen pleasures are not always the sweetest. It comes to understand that it may derive pleasure, not from courses of action that are undutiful, but from the very performance of its duty. The man whose life is well and worthily organised finds that pleasure and duty are not in eternal conflict. His life as a whole is the carrying out of his duty; but his life as a whole is a pleasant one, precisely because it is a life which is loyally devoted to duty. And this is happiness. The happy life is that in which duty is pleasant, and pleasure does not conflict with duty.

Happiness is not mere pleasure. The man or woman whose life is a ceaseless round of pleasure finds that it soon begins to pall, and the happiness which he seeks is never attained, but vanishes like a will-o'-the-wisp as he goes forward to clutch it. Happiness is not a sum or aggregate of pleasures. It is the harmony of pleasure, as it is enjoyed by the man of stable character in a purposeful life. The difference between happiness and pleasure has been admirably stated by Prof. Dewey: "Pleasure is transitory and relative, enduring only while some special activity endures, and having reference only to that activity. Happiness is permanent and universal. It results only when the act is such a one as will satisfy all the interests of the self concerned, or will lead to no conflict, either present or remote. Happiness is the feeling of the whole self, as opposed to the feeling of some one aspect of the self."[1] Happiness is never *mere* pleasure, just as unhappiness is never *mere* pain. Unhappiness may often be due to a discord of pleasures. Happiness is found in a consistent life, the pleasure of whose relaxation is harmonised with the pleasure of its work.

On the other hand, happiness is not the mere performance of duty. The mere doing of one's duty will not make one happy. Happiness depends very largely on the capacity to "make the best" of everything that comes. Happiness is largely bound up with a man's willingness to be happy. But if one does one's duty with a willingness to take pleasure in it, it gradually becomes more and more pleasant in itself. "In early youth, we are accustomed to divide life broadly into work and play, regarding the first as duty or necessity and the second as pleasure.

[1] *Psychology*, p. 293.

One of the great differences between childhood and manhood is that we come to like our work more than our play. It becomes to us, if not the chief pleasure, at least the chief interest of our lives, and even when it is not this, an essential condition of our happiness. . . . One of the first conditions of a happy life is that it should be a full and busy one. . . . An ideal life would be furnished with abundant work of a kind that is congenial both to our intellects and our characters, and that brings with it much interest and little anxiety. Few of us can command this. Most men's work is largely determined for them by circumstances, though in the guidance of life there are many alternatives and much room for skilful pilotage. But the first great rule is that we must do something, that life must have a purpose and an aim, that work should be not merely occasional and spasmodic, but steady and continuous. Pleasure is a jewel which will only retain its lustre when it is in a setting of work, and a vacant life is one of the worst of pains, though the islands of leisure that stand in a crowded, well-occupied life may be among the things to which we look back with the greatest delight." [1]

Happiness, we conclude, is the union and harmony of duty and pleasure in a well-organised life. The perfectly duteous life will be the perfectly pleasant one. All its duties will be self-imposed and willingly performed, and its leisure and relaxation will be in harmony with its comprehensive aims and aspirations.

§ 2. **The Choice of Vocation.** It will, no doubt,

[1] Lecky: *The Map of Life*, pp. 19-21.

be objected that this is an ideal which may perhaps be realised by the favoured few whose vocations are perfectly congenial, but is quite impossible of attainment to the great mass of the men and women of the world. But a little consideration will show that this objection carries very little weight. In particular, we may point out (1) that the so-called higher callings or professions differ very little, if at all, in the opportunities they afford for the union of duty and pleasure from the so-called lower callings or trades ; and (2) that it is every year becoming more possible for a boy to choose his trade or profession, and thus a gradually increasing proportion of people ought to have congenial occupations.

(1) First, then, we have to show that the so-called higher callings have no monopoly of happiness. But we must begin by frankly recognising that to two great classes of workers the attainment of happiness, as the harmony of duty and pleasure, is, unless in very exceptional circumstances, impossible.

For the sweated worker happiness is hardly possible. But it is now widely recognised that sweated labour is immoral. It is a thing which ought not to be. The laws of many lands have acknowledged this by prohibiting some of its more glaring forms. Sweated labour is no vocation at all. The moralist says it ought not to exist, and the economist admits that it need not exist.

And it must also be recognised that the unskilled casual labourer has little chance of realising the good life, so long as he remains a casual. But, in general, it is his own fault if he remains a casual. Society does not want him to be a casual. It would have more use for him as a regular labourer, and it would have still more use for him if he were a skilled workman. With the evolution of modern industry, there is less and less need of the unskilled labourer. He has every encouragement to become a skilled man; and in most progressive countries the number of unskilled labourers is every year on the decrease. It may fairly be said that no one is forced by society to become an unskilled labourer.

But it ought to be noted that "unskilled" is a relative term. Much of the work done by unskilled labourers requires a considerable amount of care and promptitude and perseverance, qualities which involve demands not only on the physical, but also on the mental and moral powers of the workman. Even mere muscular work calls for more than mere muscular energy. "Although the power of sustaining great muscular exertion seems to rest on constitutional strength and other physical conditions, yet even it depends also on force of will and strength of character. Energy of this kind, which may perhaps be taken to be the strength of the man, as distinguished from that of his body, is moral rather than physical. . . . This strength of the man himself, this resolution, energy, and self-mastery, or, in short, this 'vigour,' is the source of all progress: it shows itself in great deeds, in great thoughts, and in the capacity for true religious feeling."[1] Even the toil of the navvy may be a school of virtue.

In the various trades and professions, the opportunities of living the good life differ very little. Almost every one of them offers a vocation that is

[1] Marshall: *Principles of Economics*, p. 194.

worth fulfilling. Almost every one of them provides a walk in life in which character may be developed and duty and pleasure harmonised. It has become traditional to regard certain vocations as " higher " than others. The service of art or music or education is vaguely felt to be higher than carpentry or engineering or cooking. But all socially valuable vocations have their part to play in advancing the good of humanity, and all offer worthy lives to those who engage in them. In every one of these trades or professions, the worker may take pleasure in doing his duty, and in the great majority of cases the worker does find his deepest satisfaction in the consciousness of work dutifully done. The professions do not have a monopoly of work that is pleasant. Anyone who has been taken through engineering works of any kind, and who has entered into conversation with the workers, must have been impressed with the interest the men take in their machines and their work, and the pride and pleasure they show in explaining the mechanism and processes. The machine with which they work seems to have become a part of themselves. The workers feel that their machines have grown to know them, and they take pleasure in collaborating with these mechanical partners.

Of course, there is monotony in such work. But in what walk in life is there not monotony ? The doctor gives monotonous hours to the treatment of petty ailments, the minister finds that his parishioners are " a most monotonous lot of sinners," the lawyer's work is mostly routine of a not very exhilarating kind, and the business-man spends most of his time in the transaction of uninspiring details. And even those whose lives are considered to be the freest and most desirable, *e.g.* the artist and the musician, are not exempt from long stretches of monotonous drudgery. On the whole, such vocations are not intrinsically more pleasant than the artisan's. In the professions as well as the trades there is much drudgery and dullness. But on the whole, the activities that are called into being by the trades and professions are alike accompanied by pleasure in their exercise. The artisan takes pleasure in the skill of his hand, just as the poet takes pleasure in the skill of his mind. The activity of work and the consciousness of duty done are in both cases alike accompanied by pleasure. Pleasure and duty are harmonised in a happy life in which character is realised.

(2) But it is essential for this result that the individual should feel that the trade or profession is congenial. It must be really a vocation. He should feel the call of duty towards it, but he should also feel that his happiness consists in obeying the call. It should be a walk in life into which both duty and pleasure alike conspire to guide him. The boy has a right to *choose* the occupation to which he intends to devote himself.

It is every year becoming more possible for the average boy to select the career for which he is best fitted. However low his father's position, if the boy have capacity and ambition, he can raise himself to any level. The labourer's boy as well as the peer's carries the Prime Minister's despatch-box in his satchel. The improvement and popularisation of education, with the institution of suitable bursaries and scholarships, and the gradual breaking-down of class-distinctions, have done much to open a way for the energetic and capable boy. In quite recent times in our own country the boy naturally and almost necessarily followed the trade or profession in which his father or some other member of the family was engaged. Each occupation was chiefly recruited from the children of those already employed in it. It was almost impossible, at least in England and Ireland, for the son of the labourer to rise to any position better than his father's. But education is more and more making it possible for the boy who begins on the lowest rung of the ladder to attain the vocation for which he is best fitted.

But we should avoid thinking that there is any merit in the life of the climber as such. Many a man has fulfilled his vocation very indifferently as a minister or doctor, who might have done more for the world had he been content to be a good artisan. Every calling, however humble, offers the possibility of realising a good character and fulfilling a noble vocation ; and when once a man has chosen an occupation, it is generally his duty to " make the best of it " in the truest sense. The possibility of forming a strong character depends, in general, on identifying oneself with some *one* worthy occupation.

The question immediately arises, How is the boy or young man to know what is his vocation, and in what particular occupation he will be best able to fulfil it ? This is the most difficult practical problem that the youth is ever called upon to face. Of course, there are some boys who do not need to consider the question at all. If the boy is heir to an estate or great business, it is his duty to take the place which birth has assigned to him. And in other cases the father or mother decides for the boy what trade or profession he is to follow, and he is forced into this. But in the vast majority of cases the average boy has, within certain limits, a free choice between various possible occupations. The average boy, as we saw in Chapter VI., is fond of dallying with the thought of himself as realised in various trades and professions. He pictures himself at one time as a soldier, at another as a doctor, at another as a car-conductor, and so on. Sometimes two or three of these fancied selves, or (to put the same thing in other words) two or three of the callings that appeal to him, seem so equally desirable that a rational choice becomes almost impossible. The more similar the alternatives, the more difficult choice always is.

If the boy or young man is seriously troubled and anxious about this question, can ethics help him by suggesting any principles on which he may decide ? There is no other moral matter on which advice and guidance is more frequently sought. The teacher finds that his boys are very ready to consult him on this question, and if he is conscientious he is often puzzled what advice to give, and what principles to suggest for the guidance of the boy. Does ethics have any assistance to give ? There are three very general principles which ethics may lay down. They are all very obvious, but we are very apt to overlook them.

(1) The choice of vocation is a moral question. It is not a matter simply of expediency or profit. We

are too apt to consider that a trade or profession is desirable in proportion precisely to the money it offers. But vocation means much more than money. The life of mere money-making is not a moral vocation. We should, of course, remember that many occupations which seem at first sight to be concerned simply with money-making have a significance which transcends this. The business of stockbroking, for instance, does not have money-making as its end-all and be-all. The stockbroker performs a useful social function. Without him the wheels of the commercial world would drag, or might even refuse to move at all. The real value of the stockbroker's occupation is not the money he makes out of it, but the service he renders the community. A particular vocation is not to be assessed simply at its money value.

(2) A man should choose the occupation which he believes it is his duty to enter. It is his duty to play a worthy part in life ; it is his duty to make the most of the talents which have been committed to him ; it is his duty to use them in the particular calling in which their exercise will be most socially valuable. Owing to the principle of the division of labour, the community offers a man a very large variety of possible callings. With the advance of civilisation, the number of different occupations has risen enormously, and shows a constant tendency still to increase. In a primitive society all men are hewers of wood and drawers of water ; but gradually these functions become specialised and new ones are developed. The great increase of the division of labour depends on the fact that " practice makes

perfect." The more frequently a man does a thing, the more expert he becomes in doing it. Corresponding to this, there is the psychological fact of the specialisation of function. Certain men are more fitted by nature than others to perform certain functions. It is a man's duty to perform that function for which he is best fitted, to occupy that station in the community to which he is naturally best adapted.

(3) But a man's inclinations are also of importance in the choice of vocation. If I choose my profession or trade merely because it is my duty to do so, quite apart from the question whether I have any liking for it, it is improbable that I shall make the most of life. It is usually fatal for a man to enter an occupation, simply because he is actuated by a strong sense of duty. Unless his inclinations be in accordance with his duty, a feeling of discontent is apt to remain with him all his life. Unless we like our work, we can do neither it nor ourselves justice. In a word, the calling must be congenial.

Only if our vocations are congenial, only if duty and pleasure can be harmonised in them, can we adopt the attitude of loyalty towards them. And unless we are loyal to our vocations we cannot hope to fulfil them well. But, it may be asked, what does loyalty to vocation imply ? In being loyal to my vocation, must I practise self-denial, or may I make my vocation the means to my own self-assertion ? Does loyalty to my vocation require me to consult first the interests of others, or, since it is *my* vocation, may I regard it from the point of view of the satisfaction of my own interests ? The attempt to answer this question leads us to consider a most important ethical problem, which has frequently in the course of this book appeared above our horizon, though its explicit examination has always been postponed.

§ 3. **Self-assertion and Self-repression.** Is the moral ideal self-denial or self-affirmation? Does duty consist in the assertion of myself or the negation of myself? Am I to seek my own interests or the interests of others? Ought I to be egoistic or altruistic? This problem has given rise to as much discussion among moralists as any other.

On the one hand, there is a persistent tendency to maintain that self-denial is the highest moral ideal. It is a man's duty, on this theory, to renounce the self with all its desires and interests and inclinations. This doctrine of self-abnegation has had wide currency as a religious and moral ideal. It is prominent in Buddhism, and in many varieties of Christianity. Puritanism and Roman Catholic monasticism alike breathe its spirit. In many ethical theories also its influence is marked. We find it in Stoicism and Cynicism, and we find it in Kant. And popular moral theory (whatever popular moral practice may be) is deeply tinctured with it. The life of "self-denial" or "self-sacrifice" is popularly held to be a peculiarly noble one.

On the other hand, the doctrine that the great aim of life consists in self-development and self-assertion has never lacked adherents. From the earliest times there have been extreme individualists, both in theory and practice, who have claimed the right to develop and cultivate themselves at whatever cost to others. In our own day, Nietzsche has strongly expressed this point of view. "Unlimited self-assertion" is Nietzsche's text, and "will to be mighty" is his slogan. The spirit of this extreme individualism has pervaded much of our life and literature. Recent plays, novels, and essays all embody its teaching. On every hand single men and women and groups of men and women are asserting themselves and clamouring for their rights.

Now, English ethical writers have usually tried to mediate between these two tendencies. They have endeavoured to compromise between the two extreme attitudes. They tell us that human nature consists partly of "self-regarding" or selfish tendencies, and partly of "other-regarding" or unselfish ones. Some of our actions show the influence of "self-love," others of "benevolence." English ethics tells us, in effect, that the man whose actions are all self-regarding is a knave, and the man whose actions are all other-regarding is a fool.[1] The wise and good man is he who strikes the proper balance between them. Now probably, in practice, this is what most people actually do. The average worthy citizen, as he himself would say, indulges himself and asserts himself in certain respects, and restrains himself and denies himself in others.

But, from the ethical standpoint, compromise is not the true solution of the dispute between self-denial and self-assertion, between altruism and egoism. This will become clear if we bear in mind

[1] This is, of course, a very sweeping characterisation of English ethics, and it would need development and qualification to make it absolutely true.

the meaning of the self. The self, we insist, is social; it is the whole man, considered not as an isolated unit, but as part of a family, an organ in a body-politic, and a member of a religious community. While retaining his own individuality he merges his interests, desires, aspirations, and duties in those of the family and community of which he is a part. He identifies himself with the ends which he seeks as a loyal servant of his vocation. Thus his real self becomes his family, or his profession, or his state, or his church. When we understand self in this sense, the conflict between the adherents of self-denial and the partisans of self-assertion very largely disappears. Or at least, while the practical conflict will remain till the end of time, it is possible to reach a theoretical conclusion, which, while compromising nothing, yet recognises that, as we might expect from the persistence with which they have been defended, there is some truth in each of the opposing views. They contain truths which contribute to the truth. The truth in this matter will only be recognised if we keep clearly before our minds the meaning which we have assigned to the self.

What, then, is our conclusion? It is this. Self-denial cannot be the ultimate moral ideal. For self-denial as the absolute moral end would involve the abnegation of the *whole* self; and that is impossible. It would imply not merely the sacrifice of a man's private self, but also the renunciation of the family and the state and the church. And no apostle of self-denial has ever advocated that. However extreme an ascetic may be, he never denies the *whole* self. Ascetics have commonly renounced the family and all social and political relations, but they have done so in order to develop and assert the religious self, which for them was the widest and truest of all. Absolute self-denial is a contradiction in terms. When a man gives up everything for the sake of the kingdom of God, he does so because his self is wholly identified with the kingdom of God. He denies certain aspects of the self for the sake of the highest and most comprehensive self.

The moral ideal is the complete development and assertion of the highest and most comprehensive self, through loyal devotion to some worthy vocation. The moral ideal is thus self-assertion in the best sense; for the good man is he who does all in his power to develop and assert the comprehensive self, whether that be family or state or church, with which he has identified his nature. His own private self is felt to be a fragment, whose interests are not worth considering when they come into conflict with the good of the comprehensive self as a whole. In a well and worthily organised community the individual finds that by consulting the interests of the comprehensive self which we call family or church or state, he is at the same time satisfying his own interests, for these have been identified with those of the more comprehensive selves.

§ 4. **Loyalty to Vocation.** In thus being loyal to his vocation, he will frequently have to deny particular desires and inclinations. Self-denial (in the popular sense of the term) plays a most important part in the process of morality. The man who has identified himself with a noble cause, so that this becomes his real self, often finds that his loyalty to his vocation conflicts with the interests of his private self or with the desires of that self. In such cases it is usually right for him to "practise self-denial," not in the sense that he denies his comprehensive self; but that, in order to assert it, it is necessary to sacrifice some of the lower aspects of the self.

The moral education of character depends very largely, as we have seen, on the success with which desires are organised and harmonised. Unworthy desires have to be repressed and unworthy interests sacrificed. This is what ordinary speech means by "self-denial." Self-denial in this sense is essential to the progress of the moral life. But it is important to notice that what is denied is not the true self, but some part of the self which is conceived to be at variance with the true self. And so, when a man denies himself for the sake of his family or country or the kingdom of God, what he does is to sacrifice those interests which are private to his individual self, for the sake of that more comprehensive self (family or church or state) which in his best moments he regards as his real self.

It is this real self that is to be asserted. It is mischievous to try to assert some one fragmentary aspect of the self. If that be done, it is always at the expense of the self as a whole. Those who speak most about their rights of self-assertion in the narrow individualist sense, do not realise that the reason why the matter occupies so much of their attention is precisely that they have no self to assert. As we say, they do not know what to do with themselves. They have chosen no vocation, they have entered on no walk of life in which to realise a character. When a man identifies himself with a worthy cause, he ceases to harp on his right of self-assertion. His energies have found a socially valuable outlet : they are devoted to the service of his vocation. It is thus, and thus alone, that the self is really asserted.

Loyalty to vocation—this unites the attitudes of self-denial and self-assertion ; and this harmonises duty and inclination. In loyal devotion to vocation the self attains its highest development. But this self-assertion depends on the fact that at every stage in its moral progress the interests of the lower aspects of the self have been denied.

It is a man's duty to be loyal to his vocation. He can do no more than this ; but he should never do less. To be loyal to his vocation is a man's highest duty ; and it is a duty that every man may attempt to perform, whether he be scavenger or king. It is at once the supreme duty and the universal duty. And if the man has himself chosen his vocation, his inclinations will be consonant with his duty : it will be his truest pleasure and surest happiness to respond to the claims made upon him by the vocation which he has himself chosen.

But the completest loyalty to vocation can be rendered only by those who not only know that they have chosen their vocation, but feel that they have been chosen by it and for it. In all that we have said about vocation no reference has yet been made to this most important point. A man's vocation is not merely what he has chosen, it is also that to which he has been called. A man, then, should feel that he is *called* to discharge the obligations of his vocation. Now, by what is he called? In some cases, no doubt, he may be called by his birth or inclinations or natural capacities. The duke's heir is called by his birth to occupy his father's position. Many a boy is called irresistibly by his inclinations to a sea-faring life. And natural capacities, early developing a special bent, call one boy to be an engineer, another to be a joiner, another to be a minister, and so on.

But if we restrict the "call" to mean nothing more than this, much of the ethical flavour of "vocation" evaporates. For the word vocation has ethical and religious implications of a very important kind. "Man's vocation is to do his duty in that sphere of life to which it has pleased God to call him." In all the tale of history the most conspicuous examples of loyalty to vocation have been afforded by men who were deeply impressed by the conviction that they were called of God. They may have been mistaken in their belief, the causes to which they attached themselves may have been unworthy; but the driving power of their loyalty was derived from the conviction that they were called of God to just those tasks and no others. But it is not only in great and noble vocations that this consciousness of a divine call exerts a powerful influence. It is solidly established by the experience of generations of men and women that what would otherwise be the monotonous drudgery of a mean occupation may be ennobled and inspired by the belief that the task is being done in God's sight and is in accordance with his will.

> "A servant with this clause
> Makes drudgery divine;
> Who sweeps a room as for Thy laws
> Makes that, and the action, fine."

There are, of course, people who feel that the God of religion means nothing to them, and has no appeal to make to them. To such people the last paragraph will be foolishness and its argument a stumbling-block. This is not the place to dispute the question with them. Rather, it may be pointed out that, if they cannot feel that they are called of God, they may at least be able to feel that they are called by "that mortal God" which we call the state. Their sense of vocation may connect itself with their loyalty to the state. They may believe that their duty consists in the faithful performance of the tasks of the sphere of life which has been assigned to them by society.

The value of a sense of vocation, whether inspired by God or society, may be put in very simple terms. The important thing in life is that we should be able to feel that the work we are doing and the life we are living are of some value and significance in the world.

Now, it is sometimes easy to be possessed by the conviction that we are necessary organs in the body politic, integral elements in the life of society. During the War the shipyard worker and the engineer in the munition-factory can realise that they are necessary members of the community, and that in performing the tasks of their vocation faithfully they are contributing to the good of the state as a whole. But times come when the state seems to have no use for some of its citizens. They are "unemployed." The state has nothing for them to do. They are unwanted. They form for the time an unnecessary surplus, about which the state seems to care not at all. In such circumstances it is impossible for a man to believe that the state has a vocation for him to fulfil. For the time being, his work and his life are obviously worthless to the state.

But if his sense of vocation is based on religion, he may still believe that he is of value. He may still be upheld by the conviction that even though society seems to have no use for him, he is of infinite worth in the sight of God. Christianity has always insisted on the value of the individual soul. Every man, however humble, is called of God to some vocation which he, and he alone, can fulfil. And this is not a mere doctrine. It has been a support and encouragement to thousands whose lives would otherwise have been barren of interest and purpose, or oppressed by anxiety and failure. Their lives have been literally inspired by a sense of vocation.[1]

§ 5. **Training for Vocation.** It is obvious that the child must be trained for his vocation. But it is

---

[1] To any reader who may chance to be familiar with philosophical discussion, it will be clear that a Metaphysic of Ethics is implied in the last two or three pages. The argument of these pages might equally well have been couched in metaphysical terms. A system of Ethics necessarily drives us on to ask ultimate questions which we cannot attempt to answer without some theory of the Whole. Such a metaphysical theory underlies these pages, and also, I hope, the general argument of the book. But for the purposes of this book I have thought it well to keep Metaphysics as much as possible in the background. It is impossible, in a book of this kind, to discuss ultimate metaphysical problems in any detail; and merely to raise them without trying to thrash them out has seemed undesirable.

far from obvious whether it is any part of the work of the school to train the child for his vocation. Is education to be " vocational " or " general " ? Is it to be " technical " or " cultural " ? This is one of the most hotly disputed questions in the educational world of to-day. Within recent years many educators have advocated the introduction of vocational studies into the ordinary school curriculum, on the ground that they render school work more real and living, secure a more intense interest on the part of the child, and make the school a more useful institution.

Into the general merits of the controversy it is impossible to enter in any detail; but attention must be drawn to one or two matters of fundamental importance.

First, we must point out that it is misleading to discuss whether education should be general or vocational. The child is destined to live his life in performing the duties and enjoying the rights of his vocation; and in a very real sense all education must be vocational. All education must be directed to help the child to fulfil his vocation with the most satisfaction to himself and the greatest advantage to the community. But it is a real question whether education should be general or occupational. " Occupational " and " vocational " are not synonymous. A man's real vocation in life may be very much wider than his occupation. Or he may have two or more occupations, though he can have only one real vocation. All women certainly have vocations to fulfil, but comparatively few of them fulfil these vocations in any particular trade or profession. It is the great aim of every life to perform its function well, and it is the great duty of every life to be loyal to its vocation. Hence all education must attempt to prepare the child for the realisation of the ideals of his vocation. In order that the vocation may be fulfilled, all his life, both duty and pleasure, both business and leisure, must be organised in its service. And in so far as all education is a preparation for such a life, all education is vocational. But within vocational education, which, as we have seen, is the whole of education, we may distinguish " general " education from " occupational " education; and the question we have to answer becomes, Ought education in the elementary school to be general or occupational ?

In the elementary school occupational education should have no place. The elementary school system does not exist to turn out workmen ; it exists to turn out men. It aims at laying the foundations of character, of mental ability, and of manual skill. It is no part of its task to specialise character or intelligence or skill in any one particular direction. It must try as far as it can, in the short years at its disposal, to raise to the highest possible level the general capacities of the child. This is not to say that the work of the child in school must be exclusively book-work. Far from it. Manual work of all kinds—cookery, sewing, gardening, and so on—ought all to have a place in the curriculum of the elementary school. Now these activities are valuable, not because they have a connection with some special occupation, but because of their general educative value in training the child in alertness of mind and manual dexterity. They are not occupational studies. The object of woodwork is not to produce cabinetmakers, any more than the object of Latin is to produce professors of Latin. Education in the elementary school ought to be general.

Yet it is coming to be realised that it is part of the duty of the school to discover the kind of occupation for which the child is best fitted. The child's teacher is often appealed to for advice regarding the line of work most suited to the child's abilities; and teachers of insight have often been able to give the most valuable guidance. But in the future, psychologists maintain, it will be possible to determine scientifically the nature and strength of the child's capacities, and thus to give definite help to the child in securing that he shall enter the occupation to which he is best adapted by his natural endowment. At present, in many schools the pupil is supplied with a "personal card," on which his physical qualities are recorded in quantitative terms. There seems little doubt that in the future, when the psychologist's experiments with fatigue-tests and the ergograph prove capable of general application in elementary schools, the personal card will record also the mental characteristics of the child. By a study of the child himself, combined with a knowledge of the objective results of his physical and mental measurements, the teacher of the future may hope to be able to give him most valuable advice regarding the choice of an occupation.[1] The ele-

---

[1] On this question see Adams: *The Evolution of Educational Theory*; Brown: *The Essentials of Mental Measurement*; and Münsterberg: *Problems of To-day*.

mentary school will not itself teach occupational subjects. It will be a School of Discovery, whose task it is to understand the child and find out the particular line of his propensities and capacities.[1]

Most important of all, the school must try to instil into the child those ideals without which no true vocation is possible. Most children have ideals of some sort. " Even the dullest clod has his fairy vision. It may be a narrow, even a degrading one ; yet it is to him the light which brightens his path, for it shows him a picture which to his mind is better than the reality of his life. He may limit his hopes to sensuous pleasure, to increase of wealth, to ignoble revenge ; but the hope inspires him, whatever it may be. On the other hand, one's aspirations may soar to heaven and inspire the earnest struggle of the saint, or seek in highest art the realisation of supremest beauty, or in social service the noblest perfection of human life." [2] The school should aim at securing that the child, with his capacity for cherishing ideals, should take the highest of all as *his* ideals. If the child forms low ideals, his work will be poor, and the occupation which he chooses will be regarded by him as merely monotonous drudgery, from which he is ever seeking escape. On

[1] These remarks have reference only to the elementary school. It seems fairly clear that secondary schools and evening continuation schools should offer courses both on the lines of general cultural education, and in special occupational studies. The great difficulty in the way of the introduction of such occupational instruction is, of course, the expense of providing the numerous specialised courses that would be required. For a valuable statement of experience in Munich, see Kerschensteiner : *The Schools and the Nation.*

[2] Welton : *The Psychology of Education,* p. 412.

the other hand, if his ideals are lofty, the toil of his trade or profession will be transformed by them. He will endeavour to produce the best work possible, for only so will he be realising his ideals. No man can truly be said to have a vocation at all, unless he is trying to realise a comprehensive ideal in life. A comprehensive ideal organises all the purposes of a man, so that they do not conflict, but work together harmoniously in the fulfilling of his vocation.

For further reading: J. Seth: *Study of Ethical Principles*, pt. i. ch. iii.; J. Royce: *Philosophy of Loyalty*, ch. iii. and vi.; J. Dewey and J. H. Tufts: *Ethics*, ch. xviii.; H. Rashdall: *Theory of Good and Evil*, vol. ii. ch. iv.

CHAPTER XIV.

GOODNESS AND THE VIRTUES.

§ 1. **The Struggle of the Moral Life.** All that we have said about the moral life shows that it involves struggle. Character is not formed by drifting with the stream of life. The fulfilment of vocation requires, as we have seen, the assertion of the comprehensive self, and the denial of such private desires and interests as may be inconsistent with it. Now assertion involves energy and perseverance, and renunciation implies pain and effort. All this means struggle. Goodness of character is not attained simply by wishing or hoping or desiring or acquiescing. It requires a constant struggle: "it is hard to be good." Perfect goodness never is completely attained. But the good man is always in process of attaining. His life is a struggle in which he is gradually realising his ideals. It is impossible for a man to stand still morally. If he is not improving, or at least trying to improve, he is deteriorating. The moment he says to himself, "I have attained," he begins to fall.

Much of our moral life has, indeed, been given over to habit, and in accordance with habit we do what is right or wrong almost mechanically. In doing such habitual actions, we are not explicitly conscious of struggle. But these habits had themselves to be formed, and they were formed by the repetition of deliberate acts. In the formation of habits, as we have seen, the struggle is often fierce ; and if it be true that much or most of our moral conduct is habitual, that only means that we are now reaping reward or punishment for victories or defeats in former moral struggles. But however much of our moral life has been taken over by the automatism of habit, scarcely a day or even an hour passes without the emergence of a situation which involves moral struggle. Every day brings with it new situations and new circumstances, and however habitual our way of life may have become, we are forced to adapt it to the new conditions. Unruly desires solicit satisfaction, flitting ideas distract our attention, capricious emotions affect our equanimity. In some cases the struggle between the self and the distraction may be so slight that we are hardly aware of it at all, in others the victory may be won in a moment, for we put the intruding thought or desire from us without hesitation. In other instances the struggle may continue for days or weeks, and produce the profoundest moral anxiety. But whether the struggle be severe or not, it is in the hours of conflict that character is moulded. Goodness of character is not a talent or gift. It must be attained or achieved.

§ 2. **The Virtues, or Aspects of Goodness.** In ordinary speech a distinction is commonly observed between virtue and goodness. We talk indifferently of " virtue " and " goodness " in the abstract, but

we never say "a goodness": it must always be "a
virtue." Hence common usage encourages us to
think that we can possess particular virtues, just as
we possess clothes and houses. But a virtue is not
a particular thing like a hat or an umbrella that we
may acquire or cast away without affecting the self.
A virtue has reference to character and conduct:
it may be called adjectival to character, though such
a phrase does not emphasise nearly enough the
intimacy of its connection with character. When
we say, in ordinary speech, that a man has the
virtue of courage, we really mean that his character
and conduct are courageous. If we say that he
displays the virtue of justice, we really mean that
his character and conduct are just. The virtues, then,
are aspects of goodness. Perfect goodness is compact of all the virtues, and the perfectly good
character would be perfectly virtuous. Goodness
may appear in an infinite variety of aspects: the
man of good character will express his goodness in
actions of the most diverse kinds, and his conduct
will vary in accordance with changing circumstances.
The virtues are infinite in number. But most
moralists have found it convenient to classify them
under four heads, viz. Courage, Temperance, Justice,
and Wisdom. These are usually called the Cardinal
Virtues, *i.e.* the hinges on which all good actions
hang.[1] This classification was originally given by
Plato,[2] and though it is not free from defects, and
many other classifications have been suggested since

[1] From Latin *cardo*, a hinge.
[2] Even before his time it was anticipated by other Greek thinkers.

his time, it still remains the most satisfactory. But we should remember that such a list is simply a statement of different aspects of goodness of character and conduct. All or none of these aspects of goodness may be exhibited by an action. The same act may be at once courageous, temperate, wise, and just. In such a case all the chief aspects of goodness are possessed by it. On the other hand, a courageous act may be unwise and intemperate and unjust, and a wise action may be neither courageous nor just. It is difficult sometimes to decide whether a man's character or conduct is good, precisely because it may exhibit one or more aspects of goodness without the others.

But, in general, the man who engages seriously in the struggle of morality tends to develop all the virtues harmoniously. The cardinal virtues are systematic, and real goodness of character expresses itself equally and naturally in all of them. The good character expresses itself whole-heartedly and impartially in its actions—and that is justice; it exhibits fortitude and perseverance—and that is courage; it exercises self-control in all things—and that is temperance; and its conduct shows insight, reflection and deliberation—and that is wisdom. The virtues appear only in actual conduct. They are not inert possessions of the self. They really exist only in activity of some kind. "No man," Aristotle said, "is virtuous in his sleep." A virtue is always an activity of character, an activity exercised in some department of the struggle of the moral life. Courage could not exist, were it not for the difficult and dangerous situations which call for

GOODNESS AND THE VIRTUES

its expression. Temperance or self-control would be meaningless if man had no unruly desires and inclinations to restrain.

Every age must construct its virtues for itself. In every age character must react in new ways to the difficulties of the situations which face it. The moral life is not stationary. It is a constant progress, and the virtues in which it is expressed necessarily alter from time to time. The virtues required in one age are not those whose activity is most valuable in another. Thus we find that the precise meaning of the four cardinal virtues changes from age to age. Virtues are relative to the society in which they are displayed. The interpretation which we give to the cardinal virtues to-day differs from that which they bore in Plato's time. Yet they are fundamentally the same aspects of goodness.

The cardinal virtues are closely connected with the idea of vocation. All without exception are involved in loyalty to vocation. It might perhaps be said that while wisdom and justice are chiefly concerned with the choice of vocation, courage and temperance are mainly displayed in the process of devotion to it. But such a distinction is only a relative one, for the choice of vocation may require real courage and self-control, and wisdom and justice are constantly called for in the actual progress of the moral life.

§ 3. **Courage.** Courage is probably the first virtue to appear in the childhood of the individual and the race. The first definite quality which character develops is courage. The child and the savage learn to be brave, to bear pain and discomfort, while as yet the other virtues have not emerged. Courage may be said to be the virtue from which all the others are developed. It is significant that the word virtue is derived from the Latin *virtus*, which originally meant manliness or courage. The special virtue of man was considered to be courage, and from it all the others were supposed to have grown.

In a primitive community courage meant simply physical bravery in face of danger, but as opportunities decreased for displaying such bravery in conflicts with wild beasts and the forces of nature, and in fighting against enemies, the meaning of the virtue was gradually extended. It was recognised that mere physical boldness is not the only kind of courage, and that other callings besides warfare call for the virtue. Courage thus becomes immeasurably more comprehensive. Under the general name courage are grouped the specialised aspects in which it is manifested in various vocations. The obstacles to be faced and overcome vary in different callings, and the precise kind of courage required to meet them differs accordingly. The sailor, the soldier, the business-man, the doctor, and the minister have to face very different forms of danger and difficulty. We claim that they should show the kind of courage appropriate to their occupation, and if they fail in this, we account it a much more serious delinquency than if they are found wanting in a kind of courage that is not needed by their calling. The sailor is expected to be brave in a storm at sea, but he is not expected to tend the sick in a small-pox hospital. The soldier is expected to be unflinching in battle, which has so organised its social life that all its citizens live in harmony.

Two aspects of justice were distinguished by Aristotle—justice as distributive and justice as corrective. Distributive justice in the state demands that all men should be treated equitably in accordance with their merits. All men are not equal in capacity, and all men do not deserve equally well of the community, so distributive justice does not claim an equal distribution of goods to every man; but it does try to secure that all men shall be treated equitably and fairly. The just state will distribute goods to its citizens in proportion to their deserts.

Corrective justice becomes necessary when distributive justice has failed or has been overridden. If one citizen has obtained more than his due proportion of goods, either by such obviously unlawful means as theft or by subtler illegality or unfairness, it becomes the duty of the state to correct the disproportion. Thus justice in the strict legal sense is almost wholly corrective justice.

Justice should be understood in a sense wide enough to comprise benevolence and mercy. True justice should be so comprehensive that benevolence and mercy will become simply aspects of it. Mercy apart from justice is necessary only because justice has failed. The poor and the distressed are constantly reminding us that what they want is not mercy and charity, but justice. A true conception of moral justice would recognise that much of what is still regarded as charity or philanthropy, as works of mercy or grace, is really simply justice. Doles given to the aged poor used to be considered to be charity:

now it is realised that it is simple justice that the poor should have old-age pensions. Justice is not inconsistent with sympathy. Justice must, indeed, be impartial, and if a man allows sympathy to get the better of his judgment, he is not really just ; but an impartial sympathy is possible, and seems indeed to be of the essence of social justice.

§ 6. **Wisdom.** The virtue of wisdom should perhaps be regarded as the foundation of all the virtues rather than as a virtue in itself. There would seem to be no virtue without some wisdom or knowledge. We have pointed out that reason forms the basis of moral judgment, and that every right action involves some awareness or knowledge or conscientiousness in its performance.

The two aspects of wisdom of greatest importance in connection with virtue are insight and reflection. The wise man is the man of insight. In treating of duty, we pointed out that the value of moral rules is very limited : they must be applied by the man of insight who has a conscientious attitude to life. Moral insight is one of the most distinctive marks of the good man.

The other ethically valuable aspect of wisdom is reflection. Virtuous action is not simply a matter of insight. Morality, as we have seen, involves reflection. All good moral actions are voluntary, either in the sense that they are definitely willed, or that they are performed in accordance with habits which have been formed by the repetition of willed actions. And every voluntary action involves reflection and thoughtfulness. The virtuous man does not act in obedience to every impulse and in order to enjoy every emotion: he reflects on alternatives, and thinks over prospective courses of action, and his character is formed by reflection and thoughtfulness. Wisdom is the foundation of all virtue.

§ 7. **The Education of the Virtues.** How far is the child capable of being educated in virtue? Can the child be trained to be courageous and temperate and just and wise? Most certainly he can. The virtues, as we have seen, are simply different aspects of goodness of character, and goodness of character is acquired by training. A man's character becomes virtuous only by the habitual doing of virtuous actions. He acquires the virtue of temperance only by constantly practising self-control; and he becomes courageous by habitually acting bravely in the difficulties and dangers of life. The possibility of sound moral education depends on the fact that goodness of character is a unity; and the several virtues will develop most naturally and truly if they grow from the character as a whole. Hence the task of moral education is to train character as a whole, rather than to attempt to impose peculiar virtues on it from the outside. The education of character is on precisely the same footing as the education of the mind. It has long been recognised that education does not aim at filling the mind from the outside with knowledge, whether "useful" or "useless." Education insists that its task is to train the mind to develop its own powers by attending to and observing the world, and by assimilating what enters into its experience. Precisely the same thing is true of the education of character. The attempt to instil particular virtues from the outside is foredoomed to failure. The development of character should be an all-round development, from the centre outwards.

In particular, it is no part of the task of moral education to train the child in that specialisation or particularisation of the virtues to which we have already referred. We have seen that the virtue of courage, for instance, appears in different forms in the soldier, the teacher, the sailor, the doctor, and the worker in the explosives factory. Now the child's courage will not be developed any the better, if he knows what specialised courage these vocations require. The child's concern is primarily with such courage as he needs and is called upon to display as a child. If he learns to bear himself with courage as a child, he will not be found wanting when he is called upon to display the particular variety of that virtue which is required by the vocation which he follows. Some schemes of moral education certainly leave upon the child the impression that the virtues are needed only in after-life. Nothing could be more pernicious. The possibility of sound moral education depends upon the presumption that if the foundations of character are well and truly laid during school life, by the habitual doing of virtuous actions in those departments of life which are open to the child, the character in after-life will naturally express itself in conduct which reveals these virtues in any situation in which it may find itself.

Hence it is important to note that ordinary school life affords real and great opportunities for training in the virtues. Courage is needed by the child at the beginning of its school life, courage to leave its home, whether for a few hours or for a whole term, courage to associate with strangers, courage to face ridicule and practical joke. Courage in the form of attention and concentration is needed to overcome the initial difficulties of lessons ; and as perseverance the same virtue of courage is constantly being tested throughout the whole of school life, whether in work or at games. Courage is needed, also, to enable the child to make a stand against the force of its fellows' opinion, in schools where the tone is bad. And, of course, the child's courage may be tested also by the traditional bully, whether he be boy or teacher.

Temperance also finds a field for its exercise in the school. The child must learn to control his whims and fancies, his impulses and inclinations, all of which are probably regarded with much indulgence at home. It has always been recognised that one of the chief functions of the school is to train the child in habits of obedience and order. The child is placed under the discipline of the school, in order that he may learn how to discipline himself. School-discipline is valuable only in so far as it is really training the child to govern himself. An external authority which is not inwardly acknowledged by the child is worse than useless, because, as soon as the child secures his freedom from what he conceives to be the bonds of such an authority, reaction is apt to set in, and he will glory in showing that he can now " do as he likes." Such " doing as he likes " is simply intemperance. Discipline will fail of its lessons, unless its principles are so appreciated by the child that he will come to apply them himself in the control of his own life. And the child very early learns the necessity of self-discipline. He finds that the exhortation "Yield not to temptation" is no empty one. Temptations as real if not as violent as those of later life beset him—temptations to cheat, to tell lies, to use bad language—and in presence of such temptations he must learn to control and govern himself.

Justice is a virtue to which most children are exceedingly sensitive. The child is alert to notice any suspicion of favouritism on the part of the teacher. If the teacher pays special attention to any one pupil, the rest are apt to think that this one is a "pet," and that the teacher's attitude is "not fair." Partiality is quickly seen by the children to be inconsistent with justice. None of them want to be "pets"; but they all want to be treated fairly. The ethics of childhood is very largely based on this virtue. In the view of the child, it is wrong to carry tales, because it is "not fair"; it is wrong for a big boy to bully a small one, because it is "not fair"; it is wrong to cheat, because it is "not fair." In the child's work, as in his games, a practice is immediately and universally condemned if it is seen to be "not fair." The school offers an admirable training-ground for the child to cultivate the virtue of fairness and justice.

Little need be said of the place of wisdom in the school. The school primarily exists to teach wisdom in the best sense. It is now universally recognised in theory, however imperfectly that theory may be carried out in practice, that education which merely supplies the child with pre-digested knowledge of facts succeeds only in producing obtuseness and stupidity in the child. The aim of the school is to develop the natural insight of the child, to enable him to make the best use of the capacities with which he has been endowed, to train him in habits of observation and reflection, and to encourage him to think and reason for himself. In so far as the school is successful in this, it is helping to educate the child in virtue, for it is making it easier for him to acquire the habit of what Arnold of Rugby termed " moral thoughtfulness." And a sane moral thoughtfulness, free from cant and priggishness, is the foundation of all virtue.

For further reading : C. F. D'Arcy : *Short Study of Ethics*, part ii. ch. x. and xi.; S. E. Mezes : *Ethics*, ch. ix.-xiv.; J. Dewey and J. H. Tufts : *Ethics*, ch. xix.; T. H. Green : *Prolegomena to Ethics*, §§ 240-285.

CHAPTER XV.

THE INSTITUTIONS OF THE MORAL LIFE.

§ 1. **Morality and Social Institutions.** The moral life is essentially a social life. In the moral life, no man liveth to himself and no man dieth to himself. The earliest experience of the child is constituted by its association with other persons. The possibility of good moral conduct depends on the fact that men and women associate with one another, with a view to some end which is conceived as common and regarded as desirable, not as a private advantage, but as a public benefit. The good that is sought is a common good. In all virtuous action the end that is subserved is a common end. When a man acts courageously and temperately and wisely and justly, his action does not terminate in himself. Even when he seems to be consulting only his private advantage, his conduct necessarily has a social reference. The good that he seeks is not isolated. It may include the good of others, or it may result in the pain and misery of others. Every one of our actions, whether we wish it or not, exercises some influence on other human beings in the social community in which we live. By our conduct we help to uphold or undermine the principles on which the various social institutions are based ; and, in turn, these institutions help to mould the characters of those who are brought up in them. The most important of these institutions are the state, the family, the school, and the church. All these institutions, as we saw in Chapter III., have a firm foundation in the instinctive basis of human nature. But in their developed forms they have risen far above the merely instinctive level. As we know them, they are capable of being the centres of man's highest aspirations and noblest ideals ; and they provide the arena in which his severest moral conflicts are waged and his truest moral victories gained.

While, among these moral institutions, it is the special function of the school to undertake the conscious and deliberate education of character, all the institutions perform educative functions and have an educative value. All the institutions help to form the habits and interests of those who belong to them. Many of the specially educative functions which used to be performed by the other institutions are now being delegated to the school, or claimed by it. But the state, the family, and the church still exercise an indispensable educative influence on various departments of conduct ; and from the point of view of education it is unwise for the school to try to arrogate to itself the complete control and education of childhood. It must be recognised that all the institutions have their proper contribution to make to the education of the young ; and whatever experiments we make in education we should be careful that the school does not encroach upon the educational functions proper to the other institutions and most efficiently performed by them.

§ 2. **The State.** The most comprehensive of all moral institutions is the state. At different times and in different countries the state has been defined in very different ways. It has been taken to mean the monarch who is the actual embodiment of the power of the state, and in whose name all laws are passed and all justice administered. " L'État c'est moi." The state is also sometimes understood to mean the executive body of ministers (*e.g.* " the Cabinet "), or the particular party in power (*e.g.* " the Liberals "), or the gathering of representatives of the people (*e.g.* " Parliament "). But when we speak of the state as a moral institution, we are interpreting it in a much wider sense than that. By a state we mean an organised community of people, in which each member performs his function, exercising wisely the powers with which he is invested, and giving willing obedience to those who are set over him.

Very different views have been taken of the proper relation of the state to its individual citizens. In our own day two main views frequently come into conflict. On the one hand an extreme individualism is asserted, on the other hand is preached an extreme socialism. On the one hand there is an insistence on the rights of the individual, on the other the rights of the state are emphasised. The settlement of the controversy between socialism and individualism is one of the gravest and most pressing moral tasks which face the twentieth century. If we are to suggest lines on which the opposition between socialism and individualism may be broken down, and are to have a true conception of the proper and fruitful relations of state and citizen, we must examine briefly the meaning of socialism and individualism, and indicate the errors which they contain in the extreme form which they often assume.

Individualism emphasises the rights which the individual possesses in the state and against the state. It assumes that the individual has, to start with, a large stock of natural rights, rights to live, to work, to enjoy the produce of his work, to perform his function without molestation from other individuals or from the state itself. In particular, individualism asserts the right of liberty. Liberty, it maintains, is a natural right, and every encroachment of the state upon the private freedom of its individual citizens must be resisted to the last. It is assumed that the laws of the state and political restrictions are constantly tending to lessen the freedom of the individual; and that individual freedom is possible only if the state and its regulations are held at arms' length. In a state of nature, it is supposed, the individual is wholly free; but as social communities develop, slice after slice is cut from his freedom until hardly anything remains. An extreme individualism regards the free life of Robinson Crusoe as its ideal. Crusoe on his solitary island was free from all state interference; no social restrictions nor moral laws nor political regulations encroached upon his liberty of thought and action. He was monarch of all he surveyed.

Now a little reflection is sufficient to show the inadequacy of an individualism of this extreme type. The whole individualist theory rests on a false view of freedom. It is not true that freedom means absolute independence of all restrictions and regulations. The purpose of laws is not to encroach upon the freedom of the individual, but to constitute it, and support it. That country is most free whose laws are most comprehensive and systematic. Real freedom is unknown in a land where justice consists in the capricious sentences of caliph or sultan. Freedom is made possible for the individual by the system of laws which the state administers. The individual's freedom does not mean simply liberty to act in accordance with the whim of the moment. Rather it implies the willingness of the individual to realise his own ideals by acting in accordance with the laws which he as a citizen may have helped to pass, which he supports by his loyal obedience to them, and which, so far from infringing upon his liberty of action, alone make it possible. The state is not, as extreme individualism implies, an alien power external to the individual and constraining his obedience by force of compulsion : it is a community of which he is a member, having a common will with which his will may be at one. In being a member of his state, he implicitly acknowledges the justice of its laws, and if by his actions he incurs the penalties which these laws sanction, the sentence is in a very real sense imposed by himself. He acknowledges the justice of the laws, for they are not imposed by an external power, but by *his own* state.

Socialism is one of the vaguest words in the language, but in the form in which it is often preached it is the doctrine according to which all the means of producing wealth, land, factories, machinery, and so on, should be possessed by the state. The state, it is maintained, should delegate the use of these means of

INSTITUTIONS OF THE MORAL LIFE 225

production to individuals and groups of individuals justly and equitably; but the state itself should undertake all measures of great social importance, in order to ensure that they be carried out for the benefit, not of any one class or section of the community, but of the citizens as a whole. Socialism magnifies the office of the state and extends the range of its activities.

However lofty the ideals of such a socialism, it is apt to be defective or positively mischievous in practice. It tends to destroy the sense of personal responsibility in its citizens and weaken their initiative, energy, and individuality. If the citizens regard the state as simply an institution to do this for them and provide that for them, they will be apt to live not for the state but on the state. Such a socialism will make the citizens dependent on the state in spirit and will as well as in material circumstances.

Socialism and individualism, in the form in which they have been stated above, necessarily come into conflict. An individualism whose ideal is the jealous preservation and vigorous assertion of the natural rights of the individual resents what it regards as the encroachments of the state, and a socialism whose purpose is the extension of state enterprise at the expense of private initiative condemns any expansion of individual power.

But a true individualism does not necessarily clash with a true socialism. They are not inconsistent. A true individualism and a true socialism recognise that the interests of the state and the individual are not divergent; and that it does not follow that the more the activities of the state are extended the less room there will be for individual initiative. Quite the contrary. The more the functions of the state are enlarged, the greater the opportunities afforded for the development of the individual's capacities and powers. And the individual's interests are not inconsistent with those of the state. The more comprehensive and profound the interests of the individual, the more capable they are of promoting the good of the state as a whole.

When both state and citizens are strong, conflicts between them will be rare. On the other hand, when either state or citizens are unduly weak, constant collisions will occur. The regulations of the state will seem irksome to the citizens, and the pretensions of the citizens will seem to the state presumptuous. Both in state and citizens the sense of responsibility will be either weak or altogether lacking. But in the good and strong state it is recognised that the laws of the state supply the conditions under which the individual's best work can be done, and that the energy and initiative of the individual contribute not only to his own advantage, but also to the well-being of the state as a whole. Such state undertakings as the post office do not limit individual activity. Rather they widen the individual's sphere of legitimate enterprise, and enable him to use and organise more efficiently the means at his disposal.

A good state makes it possible for the individual to perform the function for which he is best fitted, and thus fulfil a worthy vocation. Every man has the right to choose his vocation, but the duty is laid upon every man to fulfil that vocation to the best of his ability. Thus, both rights and duties are involved in the fulfilment of vocation in the state. The individual has a right to follow some worthy occupation in the state; but he is under an obligation to render good service in that vocation. The state is under an obligation to provide its citizens with opportunities of finding worthy callings and working in them; but it has the right to demand that they shall not abuse these opportunities. Hence rights and duties are strictly correlative. No individual has any right which does not imply a duty; and every obligation the state enforces involves duties which it cannot refuse to perform. The individual citizen claims as a right that his house should be protected from burglary and his country from invasion. But these rights imply the duties of paying rates to his municipality and taxes to his country, and, if need be, of giving personal military service in its defence. Conversely, when the state claims as a right that its citizens should pay taxes and give service, it recognises that it is its duty to advance, as far as in it lies, their legitimate interests. It is no mere form of words that appears on the passport to which the humblest citizen is entitled: "These are to request and require in the name of His Majesty all those whom it may concern, to allow . . . to pass freely and without let or hindrance, and to afford him every assistance and protection of which he may stand in need." The state as a whole stands behind its meanest citizen. It guarantees his rights and encourages him in the performance of his duties. All duties and all rights are relative to society, and are maintained by it.

§ 3. **The Family.** Within the comprehensive unity of the state the most important moral institution is the family. Though—or perhaps because—it is narrower than the state, its influence is often more profound and intense. The family is the first moral institution with which the child comes in contact, and for most children the family is the primary school of character. From his earliest hours the child begins to learn the lessons that his family has to teach; and the kind of character he forms depends very largely on the sort of influences the family brings to bear upon him.

The members of a good family form a most intimate social unity. They develop a real common will, and seek a common good. They share the same joys and feel the same griefs. They seek common ends whose realisation is made possible only by a common life which involves mutual self-sacrifice. The authority of the family used to be centred legally in the father. To him belonged absolutely all the property of the family; and he possessed the right of life and death over its members. But gradually it was realised that the will of such a family was not really a common will, and its purposes were not directed to the attainment of really common ends. The family has evolved towards a real community of will and spirit by granting more rights and privileges to wife and children. The extension of rights to members of the family other than the father has greatly increased the complexity of family life, but, while it leaves more room for conflict and discord within the circle, it also provides immensely enhanced opportunities for the formation by the younger members of the family of a real common will with united interests and a social consciousness. Property can be possessed by the various members of the family individually, but it is not usually regarded by them as *mine* and therefore not *thine*. It can be both *mine* and *thine*. It is seen to be for the use of the family as a whole. And the family property is seen to be *ours*, to be employed by us in satisfying our common needs, and in seeking the common ends in which our private inclinations and interests have been merged.

Hence there is very little truth in the charge that the family is apt to produce selfishness. No doubt a family whose outlook is restricted and whose sympathies are narrow may be selfish as a family and may encourage selfishness in its members. But such selfishness is the exception. Even when the family as a social unit is selfish, it may foster unselfishness in its members. The family circle is a small one, and its members come into such close and intimate relation to one another, that unless they practise unselfishness and forbearance, the family could not exist at all. From one standpoint, the narrowness of the family, so far from being a defect, is one of its chief excellences. It concentrates the emotions and sentiments of its members in a centre of sympathy. This unity of feeling is very clearly seen when a special joy or sorrow falls upon any one member of the family. The family as a whole shares the joys and sorrows of any of its members: an injury to one is felt as an injury to all; if one brings disgrace upon himself, it is a disgrace to the family as a whole; if one wins success and honour, the whole family rejoices, not merely because of its pride in him, but because it feels that some at least of the credit belongs to it.

In the family the reciprocal relation of rights and duties becomes clearly manifest. The relation between parents and children is one of mutual responsibility. It has been said that in the family of past time the rights of parents and the duties of children were emphasised, while in the family of the present day the rights of children and the duties of parents are prominent. Though there is some truth in this, it is truer that we are only beginning to realise the full implications of the mutual responsibilities involved in family life. We are only gradually coming to understand the extent of the duties of parents to their children and of children to their parents.

As an educative institution the family is the nurse of virtue. Goodness is taught not only by precept, but by the example of mother and father and brothers and sisters. The child learns much from the conversation that takes place in the family circle, his curiosity is stimulated, he asks questions, acquires information, and begins to take up an attitude to life. But, since the influence of the family may not be a good one, the family may also become the foster-mother of many of the vices. The early nurture that we receive in the family is probably a more potent influence for good or evil than anything else in our lives. The family teaches the preciousness of mutual affection and the value of common purposes and ideals. The relation of parents to children is so intimate that the parents ought to know far better than outsiders can in what cases the child should be encouraged to bear his own burdens, and in what circumstances a stronger and wiser hand should lend assistance. The parents ought to know where the child needs to learn the lesson of self-help, and where the duty of mutual assistance should be advised and exemplified.

One important result of this educative process is the development of the individuality of the child. To strangers the child may seem just like any other child; but to his parents he is unique: he is "like his dear self alone." The growth of his individuality is largely influenced by the intense affection and interest with which his early steps are guided.

At present, owing to a variety of causes, the family seems to be in danger of losing its fitness to help the child in the task of character-building. These causes are partly economic. Self-help is not so necessary and not so possible in the family of to-day as it was a century ago. Prof. Dewey speaks of the time, only one or two generations ago, "when the household was practically the centre in which was carried on, or about which were clustered, all the typical forms of industrial occupation. The clothing worn was for the most part not only made in the house, but the members of the household were usually familiar with the shearing of the sheep, the carding and spinning of the wool, and the plying of the loom. . . . Practically every member of the household had his own share in the work. The children, as they gained in strength and capacity, were gradually initiated into the mysteries of the various processes. It was a matter of immediate and personal concern, even to the point of actual participation. We cannot overlook the factors of discipline and of character-building involved in this : training in habits of order and of industry, and in the idea of responsibility, of obligation to do something, to produce something in the world. There was always something which really needed to be done ; and a real necessity that each member of the household should do his own part faithfully and in co-operation with others." [1] In the modern family all this has been changed. It is often very difficult for the child to find any way in which his help will be of real use to the family, and it is consequently often very difficult for him to conceive the common purposes of the family. The community of will and purpose in the modern family is as real as ever it was, but because it is now so purely spiritual a thing, it is harder for the child to recognise its reality.

And there are other causes of a vague social kind which are affecting the efficiency of the family as a moral institution. "Thirty years ago, the large majority of women could enter upon their married life with the confidence of experience, gained as part of the usual equipment of their normal home surroundings. To-day, it is lamentably, almost ludicrously, frequent to find girls of twenty-one who have never washed an infant, cut out a night-gown, or passed disturbed nights with a teething youngster. There is a natural reluctance to perform duties with which we are unfamiliar ; and the feeling of dislike, the sense of almost impotent despair with which many of them regard the possibility of having to undertake such offices, is a speaking comment on our present system of higher education for women." [2]

[1] J. Dewey : *The School and Society*, pp. 22-24.
[2] W. C. D. and C. D. Whetham : *Heredity and Society*, p. 91.

The result of this is, that the mother is only too ready to relegate the care of the infant to a nurse. The child sees very little of its mother or father; it is in the family, but not of it. Such a family as this consists really of the parents alone : to all intents and purposes the children are outside it.

For these and other reasons, the family is more and more becoming inadequate as an educative institution, and the functions which it ought to perform are more and more being transferred to the school. This process is taking place in all grades of society. At the top of the social scale, children are packed off to a preparatory boarding-school at a very early age ; at the lowest levels the child is provided for outside the home in crèches and kindergarten schools, and is often fed, clothed, and supplied with books by the educational authorities. To an ever-increasing extent the school is being forced to undertake the responsibility of the education of the characters of the nation's children.

§ 4. **The School.** With singular unanimity educators affirm that the ultimate aim of the school is the education of character. "That it should train character is one of the very few general statements about education which meet with universal assent." [1] The English code claims that elementary education should aim at the training of character. "The teachers," it says, "can do much to lay the foundations of conduct. They can endeavour, by example and influence, aided by the sense of discipline that should pervade the school, to implant in the children habits of industry, self-control, and courageous per-

[1] Welton : *Psychology of Education*, p. 463.

severance in the face of difficulties : they can teach them to reverence what is noble, to be ready for self-sacrifice, and to strive their utmost after purity and truth ; they can foster a strong sense of duty, and instil in them that consideration and respect for others which must be the foundation of unselfishness and the true basis of all good manners ; while the corporate life of the school, especially in the playground, should develop that instinct for fair play and for loyalty to one another which is the germ of a wider sense of honour in later life." [1]

This comprehensive aim cannot be realised unless the teachers are dominated by a conviction that the purpose of the school *is* an ethical one, and that they are fulfilling their vocation truly only in so far as they are helping their pupils to become upright members of the community in which they live, and worthy citizens of the country to which they belong. And they cannot do that unless they are themselves men and women of character, whose conduct corroborates the lessons they attempt to teach. "The teacher must be so penetrated with the ethical nature of his task, and so governed in all he does by the ethical aim of his vocation as giving life and significance to all he teaches and all he does, that he cannot fail to mould the thoughts of his pupils to those high conceptions of duty, justice, humanity, and religion, which are the bond of society and the sole guarantee of its stability and progress. He must, in short, himself be dominated by ethical passion ; and both the subjects taught and the methods pur-

[1] *Code of Regulations for Elementary Day Schools in England.*

INSTITUTIONS OF THE MORAL LIFE 235

sued must be regarded by him as instruments for attaining an ethical result." [1]

Granted, then, that the ultimate purpose of the school is an ethical one, and that the teachers must themselves be men and women of character, it must now be asked, How is the school to perform this task of moral education ?

On this question there are two sharply contrasted views, which have divided the educational world into two opposed camps. One party holds that the ends of moral education are most effectively promoted by *moral instruction*, the other that moral education, to be of any value, must be either primarily or wholly *moral training*. The aim of moral training is to help the child to form good habits of conduct ; moral instruction seeks to give the child right ideas about conduct. Moral training insists that the important thing in life is that the child should as a matter of fact act rightly. Moral instruction claims that the child should not only act rightly, but should know why he acts rightly.

This difference in aim is reflected in the different methods advocated by the two parties. Moral training is essentially indirect, moral instruction is direct.

Moral training is secured by the discipline of the school, maintained by the authority of the teacher and senior scholars ; by the duties and responsibilities which the older children assume in organised school games ; by the manifold influences of the corporate life of the school ; and by the disciplinary and inspiring effect of the studies of the

S. S. Laurie : *Institutes of Education*, p. ix.

school curriculum. By making use of all these instruments for moral training, the wise teacher may exercise an influence, all the more profound because the child is unconscious of it, on the formation of his pupil's character.

On the other hand, moral instruction gives definite information and exhortation on definite points, and looks for definite results. It believes in the importance of knowledge, and holds that the best way to direct the child's conduct is to tell him what is right and what is wrong, and why it is right and why it is wrong. Moral instruction may be given in different ways and on different occasions, but it is always definitely *instruction*. It may be given as a formal lesson at a regular hour, or as an informal talk as occasion arises, or in an incidental word or two in connection with some historical character or fact, or it may be veiled in parabolic form in story or poem. But in all cases alike the aim is to educate the child's character by giving him right ideas about conduct.

Now, many theorists set up these two views in sharp opposition to one another, some insisting on the value of *moral training*, others maintaining that *moral instruction* is of greater importance. But it is quite unnecessary, and may be highly mischievous, to state the issue as " moral training *versus* moral instruction." In practice, we are not confined to one of the two alternatives. We need not make an irrevocable decision to stake all *either* on moral training *or* on moral instruction. Both are necessary to moral education, and the methods advocated by both may therefore be employed.

INSTITUTIONS OF THE MORAL LIFE 237

In most schools there is some moral instruction. In many cases regular periods are set aside on the school time-table at which the teacher gives lessons on temperance, thrift, hygiene, and good manners. In other cases the headmaster has "talks" to gatherings of the children in his school. But in most schools instruction is given, not according to a pre-arranged scheme, but incidentally as occasion offers. While much controversy still rages as to the best methods of imparting moral instruction, there is practical unanimity that direct moral instruction in some form should be given. This was established by the important and representative committee which was appointed in 1907 to conduct an international inquiry into the influence of education upon character and conduct. Their elaborate report, issued under the title *Moral Instruction and Training in Schools*, embodies the result of much patient investigation of the practice and theory of moral instruction throughout the world, and contains the recommendation that direct moral instruction should be given in all public elementary schools.

In the attempt to give moral instruction, two mistakes have to be avoided. (1) The moral lesson should not be made to seem the same as any other lesson. While the teacher should certainly follow some plan in giving his course of lessons, they will have most influence on the children if the teacher attaches them to some "text," *e.g.* some important or striking event in the school or neighbourhood or state. If this be done, the lessons are much more likely to strike home than if they simply issued from a cast-iron scheme. But while the lessons will be all the more effective if they appear to be informal and incidental, there should be system in the teacher's mind. The teacher should have clearly before his mind's eye at the beginning of the session what he wants to teach the children, and should constantly ask himself, "Am I succeeding in teaching what I intended to teach?"

(2) The teacher should also remember that merely to impart knowledge about right and wrong and good and evil is not moral instruction. The comparative failure of moral instruction in France has been due almost entirely to the fact that this apparently obvious truth has been overlooked. In his sympathetic report on moral education in France, Mr. Harrold Johnson, Secretary of the Moral Instruction League, says, " No child need leave the French public primary school in ignorance of the fundamental moral distinctions. And so far this is excellent. But one is not always so sure that he leaves with firmly embedded moral principles and with any considerable driving power towards good. Moral instruction of a kind he has. Has he not committed to heart hundreds of *résumés* of moral lessons ; repeated hundreds of them word for word ; inscribed countless maxims in his copy-books ; composed numerous compositions on all the virtues ; gazed daily on mottoes on the blackboard and the walls ; copied them in the writing-lesson—by every means, at every hour, has he not had moral facts impressed on his memory, even if they have not penetrated deeper into his constitution?" [1] If these are the only results moral instruction has to show, it stands self-condemned.

[1] *Moral Instruction and Training in Schools*, ii. 17.

French moral teaching is too artificial. It has no point of contact with the actual life of the child. Now, if the teacher knows his children, he can make the moral lesson really touch their lives. The pupils should be made to realise that the moral lesson is concerned not with abstract distinctions, but with the actual task of " fighting the good fight," in which they are all engaged.

Moral education should seek to secure that the child not only knows what is right and what is wrong, but that he learns to love what is good and hate what is evil. In the struggle of the moral life we should not merely know what we fight for, but should love what we know.[1] Though we may agree that " evil is wrought by want of thought as well as by want of heart," yet it is also true that a man will never do his best in the moral struggle unless his heart is in the fight.

In order that moral principles may not remain simply facts known, but may become dynamic forces in conduct, moral education must, in addition to proceeding by way of instruction, make use of every means of actual moral training.

We have seen, in former chapters, how the instincts and impulses and desires of the child may be controlled and directed, how his emotions and sentiments may be developed and organised, how his will may be trained and his conscience enlightened. These aspects of moral education have already been

[1] Cf. Cromwell in his letter to Sir William Spring : " I had rather have a plain russet-coated Captain that knows what he fights for and loves what he knows, than that which you call a ' gentleman ' and is nothing else. I honour a gentleman that is so indeed " (Carlyle : *Cromwell's Letters and Speeches*, i. 147).

dealt with at length, and we mention them again only to emphasise that in all these ways the growing self of the child *is* undergoing moral training.

The moral training of the child is furthered by the corporate life of the school of which he is a pupil. Though " corporate life " has a very vague sound, and would be very difficult to define, it exercises an influence that is all the more pervasive because it so often operates subtly and imperceptibly. The corporate life of the school is part of the child's social environment. The social environment as a whole affects the child intensely and profoundly; but when its forces are focussed in the narrow but most vigorous life of the school, its influence becomes strictly incalculable. From the corporate life of the school, which includes all that we mean by its " spirit " or " tone " or " tradition," the child adopts the conventions that determine his moral standards; and his moral ideals are apt to be high or low in proportion as the ideals expressed in the corporate life of the school are high or low. The corporate life of the school, maintained by the scholars and fostered by the teachers, not only influences the children in the formation of their moral ideals and the adoption of their moral standards, but helps to train them in the application of these standards and the realisation of these ideals, by granting them certain responsibilities for the maintenance of school discipline and the preservation of school honour.

As a factor in the training of character the ordinary school curriculum is also of importance. The course of studies as a whole, if it be well planned

INSTITUTIONS OF THE MORAL LIFE

and the subjects well taught, ought to be the means of exerting an influence on character. But from the ethical standpoint, certain parts of it are of peculiarly great significance. It is obvious that literature and history, drawing and music, and manual activities are all capable of exercising a great influence on the development of character. It is a mistake to ask, Which has the *greatest* influence ? Their influence is greatest when they are all present, for each subject has its special contribution to make to moral training. In the study of literature and history, the child's attitude is passive and receptive ; it receives passively the ideals which literature and history have to teach it. On the other hand, in manual activity the mind is active and re-creative. It strives to express its ideals, to reproduce them in tangible and visible form, to impose its will on wood or stone or marble. And in drawing and music both these attitudes are present together. On the one hand, the mind is passive and receptive in so far as it allows the melody of a piece of music or the beauty of a landscape to impress it ; but active and re-creative in so far as it seeks to express the melody it has heard or the composition it has read or the beauty it has seen —to express them in beautiful sounds or lines or colours. These studies are morally valuable, not merely because they educate eye and ear and mind and will, but because they educate them not disproportionately but harmoniously.

But the most potent factor in all moral education has still to be mentioned. It is the personality of the teacher. The teacher can scarcely hope to exert an influence on the hidden springs of conduct of his pupils, unless he possesses the mysterious power of personality. Mysterious it is, like everything great and real; but though it is more easily felt than defined, some of the elements which go to constitute it may be mentioned. It includes a generous sympathy, combined with an acute moral insight; tact and prudence, combined with frankness of spirit and candour of heart; a sense of fairness and justice manifested in self-discipline and in a genuine respect for the rights and the infirmities of others; and, above all, a consciousness of vocation. The personality of the teacher is centred in his sense of vocation. A reasoned enthusiasm for education and a conviction of its value, a firm faith in goodness and in the possibilities of training in goodness, lofty ideals which repeated disappointment and failure cannot shatter, and a whole-hearted loyalty to the cause to which he has dedicated his life—these, and nothing less than these, are the essential qualities of the teacher who hopes to exercise an influence on the development of character.

But the best teacher is the first to recognise that the school cannot do everything. While the concentration of the school on moral education does give special power to its work, it is, after all, only one of the institutions by which the child is influenced; and it is only when it is leagued with the others that it performs its own proper functions most effectively. In particular, the school looks to the church for assistance in the task of inspiring children with noble ideals, and furnishing them with a real driving power towards good. The religious spirit may be present in the school; indeed the power of many

INSTITUTIONS OF THE MORAL LIFE

schools has been due largely to their strong religious atmosphere; but, in general, religious influences must be supplied by the church.

§ 5. **The Church.** The church differs in an important respect from the institutions which we have already considered. It is a voluntary society, and a man may be a member of it or not, as he pleases. A man not merely chooses to be an adherent of some particular religion, and a member of some particular denomination, he chooses whether or no he will be connected with any religious society at all. But participation in the activities of all the other institutions is obligatory. The child must be a member of some family, and a national of some state; and when he is old enough he must go to some school. The family, the school, and the state are institutions under whose influence he is bound to come.[1] But with the church it is different. Unless his parents have chosen to associate themselves with some religious society, the child will never receive that training which the church is peculiarly well fitted to give. There can be little doubt that the child who is debarred from learning the lessons which the church has to teach is being severely handicapped for the struggle of the moral life. At all times the church has exercised a profound moral influence; and that in two ways.

(1) The church has done more than all the other institutions put together to cherish lofty ideals, ideals which are capable of becoming in the characters of those who are inspired by them, not the empty visions of a day-dream, but dynamic forces

[1] Exceptional cases are possible.

with a real driving power towards good. There is all the difference in the world between sentimental visions and operative ideals. A sentimental vision is blind to reality, and seeks to live in an unreal realm from which all evil and misery have been excluded. But an operative ideal is firmly founded in the bedrock of things as they are. Yet it recognises that this is not the best of all possible worlds, and it is convinced that all moral progress consists in the attempt to attain an ideal goal. The ideal is itself the force which demands loyalty to its claims, and which directs the whole process of the moral life. It supplies motives for conduct, it is an incentive to action, and, though it is never completely realised, it is the source of all man's moral endeavour. Such an ideal, loyalty to which is suffused with a passionate enthusiasm for the good and the true, is rarely found in one who has not been influenced by the church. Religious ideals are not only more intense and dynamic than others, they are also more comprehensive. A noble enthusiasm for humanity organises a man's life as a whole, and inspires his every thought and deed to be serviceable to its comprehensive ends. His interests become unified, and his purposes systematic, for all are regarded as having worth only in relation to his governing ideal.

(2) In particular, the vital church inspires its members by precept and by example with the spirit of loyal service. Whenever the church fails to inculcate the duty of loyal service, it ceases to deserve the name. The church consists of those who believe that they possess " good news " of incalculable value ; and it is not a real church unless it

seeks to enlist all its members in the service of
"the good cause of the world." This is service and
the highest kind of service.

The reason why the church is so successful in
instilling the spirit of service is not far to seek. It
demands loyalty, not to an abstract idea or to a
vague cause, but to a Person. Now the child (and
not only the child) naturally tends to personify its
ideals. While an ideal in the abstract has no meaning for it, a person excites its interest, claims its
respect, and influences its actions. Hence the child
is readily attracted to such an ideal figure as Jesus,
and willingly takes up an attitude of personal loyalty
to him. Jesus appeals to the child as a real person,
whose ideal character is framed in a setting of
common incidents and familiar situations. This
person, the child is taught, claims from it loyal
service, which need not be given in any special
calling, but may be rendered in performing the
duties of any worthy occupation. For the world is
the scene of a great struggle between the forces of
evil and the powers of good ; and on this field no
post is secular.

In the past, the church has deserved well of the
world for the loyal service it has animated ; and
to-day more than ever before we need to learn the
lesson it has to teach. Such ideals as those of
" humanitarianism " or " social service," noble as
they are, have conspicuously failed, when divorced
from religion, to elicit any considerable wealth of
loyal service. The church, with all its weaknesses
and faults, still enjoys a unique power, and sustains a
unique responsibility as the institution which, above

all others, inspires men and women with the noblest ideals, and stimulates them to work them out in the activities of loyal service.

§ 6. **Moral Progress and Optimism.** For thousands of years these moral institutions, the church, the state, the school, and the family, have been in existence ; and sometimes we feel a doubt whether, after all, the toil of ages has not been in vain. Have these institutions succeeded in raising the general level of character and improving the general conditions of life ? Can we indulge any sure and certain hope that the work of education will be increasingly fruitful ? Or is the apparent progress of the world illusory ?

The question whether there has been moral progress in the past is a question of fact. On the whole, it is generally agreed that if we survey the history of the world as a whole, it is possible to trace a general movement, which, in spite of many reactions and retrogressions, has been one of moral advance. The great moral institutions are in many respects more powerful than ever they were, and on the whole they maintain with greater equity than in any previous age the rights and duties, the privileges and obligations, of their members.

But even those who would be inclined to deny that the world has seen any real moral progress are prepared to admit that in all the tale of history, discouraging as it often is, there is nothing to prevent us cherishing the hope that the future will be better than the present. We have a right to this hope, and it is only as this hope becomes an ideal to inspire our work, that we can render our best service. Only the optimist can give loyal and whole-hearted service.

Unless a man believes in the value of his work and the future of his cause, he cannot throw himself with all his energy into the tasks of his vocation.

But it is well to remember not merely that we have a right to be optimistic, but that optimism is imposed upon us almost as a duty. For optimism is a kind of courage. True optimism does not consist in building castles in the air and hiding like an ostrich from things as they are. Such a combination of sentimentality and timidity is removed by the world's breadth from true optimism. True optimism does not refuse to look facts in the face, nor does it indulge in futile day-dreams. It recognises the evil and misery in the world, it is conscious of ignorance and failure and sin, but it believes that its ideals are capable of being progressively realised in the world as it is. The optimistic man is perfectly courageous: optimism has been called " the horizon of courage." He is not deterred by the obstacles and hazards which he perceives in the path of moral progress. And when he fails, as often he must, in the moral struggle, his failure does not fill him with despair. Rather, it becomes the incentive to a fresh determination and renewed effort. It is " the sting that bids not sit, nor stand, but go."

Such an optimism is peculiarly necessary to us as teachers. For, though in no profession is it possible to have higher ideals, in none is it easier to be content with low ones. When we see how very inadequately some of those who cherish lofty ideals of their vocation succeed in fulfilling its tasks, and when we have ourselves conspicuously failed in achieving the great results for which we had hoped, we are very apt to "lose heart," become pessimistic and cynical, and decide to rest content with doing the minimum of work and securing mediocre results. It is then that a courageous optimism is necessary. For such an optimism means a refusal to acknowledge defeat, it involves a conviction that human nature is infinitely capable of improvement, and it is inspired by faith and hope that, if loyal service be rendered, failure will not always be its meed.

For further reading : C. F. D'Arcy : *Short Study of Ethics*, xii. and xiii.; Helen Bosanquet: *The Family*, x. and xiii. ; J. Dewey : *The School and Society*, i. and ii. ; J. H. Muirhead : *The Service of the State*, i.-iii. ; J. R. Seeley : *Ecce Homo*, iii., vii., ix., xi., xiv., xvi. ; Sir Henry Jones : *Idealism as a Practical Creed*, vi. and vii. ; Graham Wallas: *The Great Society*, xi.-xiii. ; Sir Henry Jones: *The Principles of Citizenship;* G. A. Johnston : *Citizenship in the Industrial World*, i., iv. and v.

INDEX

Aboulia, 108.
Acquired characters, 20-22.
   and responsibility, 32.
Acquisitiveness, 46, 50, 54.
Adams, J., 99, 202.
Alchymist of Character, 74.
Altruism, 191 ff.
Ambition, 66, 186, 246-248.
Ancestral Inheritance, Law of, 17.
Anger, 67, 71, 73, 74.
Aristippus, 168.
Aristotle, 55, 102, 103, 126, 208, 213.
Authority of Duty, 162-164.
   of law, 163, 217.
   of reason, 138.

Bad. *See* Evil.
Bain, A., 94.
Baldwin, J. M., 87, 138, 152.
Behaviour, Instinctive, 41-56.
   and conduct, 56, 121.
Benevolence, 192, 213.
Bentham, J., 146, 169, 172, 173, 174.
Bosanquet, H., 248.
Brown, W., 202.
Burnet, J., 55, 116.
Butler, 110, 116.

Character an acquisition, 27, 205.
   and conduct, 6, 117 ff.

Character and emotion, 67 ff.
   and God, 5.
   and knowledge, 5, 214 ff.
   and pleasure, 5, 177-179.
   and responsibility, 30-34.
   and sentiment, 79, 149.
   education of. *See* Education.
   groundwork of, 14-116.
   realisation of, 117-248.
   measurement of, 55, 202.
Child and convention, 131.
   and family, 228-233.
   and imitation, 86, 128.
   and moral judgment, 128 ff.
   and opposition, 87, 129.
   and perseverance, 107.
   and sanctions of morality, 150-152.
   and school, 233-243.
   and virtues, 215-219.
   and vocation, 199-204.
   education of, 35 ff., 124 ff.
   emotions of, 69, 72, 78.
   ideals of, 203, 245.
   impulses of, 58.
   instincts of, 42 ff.
   personality of, 97 ff., 125, 231.
   relation to duty, 126, 154, 162.
   relation to heredity and environment, 14 ff., 33.
   self of, 39, 83 ff.
   sentiments of, 78.

Choice, 105 ff.
　of vocation, 182-191, 202.
Christianity, 191, 199.
Church, 93, 120, 147, 243-246.
　instinctive basis of, 50-51.
Companionship, 38, 228, 240.
Conduct, 6, 117-248.
　and behaviour, 56, 121.
　and character, 117 ff.
　and the school, 124 ff.
　implications of, 122-124.
　motives of, 140-145.
　sanctions of, 145-152.
Conscience and impulse, 60.
　and moral judgment, 127, 139 ff.
　and the self, 100-102, 109 ff.
　as feeling, 110-112.
　as reason, 110-112.
　conflicts of, 112 ff.
　education of, 114 ff.
Conscientiousness, 115, 166, 214.
Consequences as test of right and wrong, 139 ff., 174.
Convention, 131-133, 147.
Courage, 207, 209-211, 216-217.
Cromwell, 136, 239.
Curiosity, 46, 50, 53-57.

D'Arcy, C. F., 219, 248.
Decision, 96, 105 ff.
Degeneration, 20.
Deliberation, 104, 106, 115.
Desire, 61-66, 194.
　and ambition, 66.
　and duty, 155, 162.
　and impulse, 61.
　and the self, 65, 195, 211.
　and will, 102, 211.
　conflict of, 61, 104, 195, 206.
　education of, 62-64, 103, 211.
　object of, 174-177.
Dewey, J., 13, 99, 116, 126, 152, 179, 181, 204, 219, 232, 248.

Discipline, 125, 211, 217, 231, 240.
Dugdale, R. A., 24.
Duties, particular, 165-166.
　relative to rights, 227, 230.
Duty, 153-166.
　and desire, 155.
　and happiness, 181, 196 ff.
　and impulse, 155.
　and interest, 154 ff.
　and the self, 164-166.
　and vocation, 189, 196 ff., 227.
　authority of, 162-164.
　child's definition of, 126, 154.
　rules of, 156-162.

Education, Moral, 7-10, 221, 233-243.
　and conduct, 124 ff., 215 ff.
　and environment, 37, 221.
　and heredity, 35.
　and ideals, 203, 242-248.
　and impulses, 58-60.
　and instincts, 51-55.
　and responsibility, 33, 125, 217.
　and sanctions, 150 ff.
　for vocation, 199-204.
　of conscience, 114-116.
　of desires, 62-64.
　of emotions, 72-77.
　of personality, 97-99, 231.
　of sentiments, 80-82.
　of virtues, 215-219.
　of will, 103, 105 ff., 215 ff.
Edwards, Jonathan, 25.
Egoism, 191 ff.
Emotion, 67 ff.
　and character, 67, 133, 142.
　complex, 68.
　simple, 69.
Environment and Heredity, 14-40.
　physical, 21-23.
　social, 27-30, 86, 90, 220, 240.

INDEX

Enthusiasm, 79, 242.
Epicureans, 168-170.
Ethics and Moral Education, 7-10.
  definition of, 1-7.
  etymology of, 6.
  relation to other sciences, 7-9.
Evil, 27, 30-34, 38-39, 52-56, 62-65, 72-82, 93-96, 103, 107-109, 118-120, 145-152, 174-179, 215-219, 230.
Example, 33, 37, 230.

Family, 228-233.
  and moral judgment, 128 ff.
  instinctive basis of, 47, 51, 221.
Fear, 45, 69, 71, 210.
Feeling, 79, 83, 140, 142.
  and conscience, 111, 112.
  as pleasure, 167, 175.
  as standard of moral judgment, 133 ff.
Freedom, 122, 223-224.
Froebel, 98, 99, 124.

Galton, Sir F., 17.
Geddes, P., 18, 22, 40.
Germ-plasm, 18, 19.
God, 5, 93, 163, 194, 197-199.
Good, 2, 8-10, 27, 30-34, 38, 52-56, 62-65, 72-82, 89, 93-96, 103, 107-109, 118-120, 145-152, 174-179, 194 ff., 205 ff., 246-248.
Good-for-man, 4-6. *See also* Good *and* Ideal.
Grahame, K., 88.
Green, J. A., 66, 73.
Green, T. H., 66, 165, 166, 219.
Gregariousness, 46, 48, 53.

Habit and character, 120, 151, 206, 215.
  and the self, 94 ff., 109, 115.

Habit, ethical maxims of, 94-96.
Happiness, 169, 183.
  relation to pleasure, 180 ff.
  relation to duty, 180 ff.
Health, Moral, 27, 54-56, 166, 181, 211.
Hedonic tone, 167.
Hedonism, 168 ff.
Herbart, 97.
Heredity and Environment, 14-40.
  mental, 24-27.
  moral, 24-27, 86.
  physical, 16-21.
History, 37, 81, 241.
Hobhouse, L. T., 44.
Hope, 67, 70, 246-248.
Horne, H. H., 40, 82.
Hume, 111.
Hutcheson, 111.
Hygiene and Ethics, 7-9.

Ideal, the Moral, 174-177, 193-199.
Ideals, 203, 221, 242-248.
Imitation, 86, 128.
Impulse, 57 ff.
  control of, 58-60, 142.
Individualism, 191, 222-226.
Individuality. *See* Personality
Insight, 55, 166, 214.
Instinctive Behaviour, 41-56.
  and emotion, 70.
  and environment, 43.
  and heredity, 42.
  and ideals, 41.
  and impulse, 57.
  and institutions, 47-51, 221.
  and reflex actions, 43.
Instincts, education of, 51-55.
Institutions, Moral, 47-51, 221-248. *See also* Church, Family, School, State.
Instruction, Moral, 38, 235-239. *See also* Education.
Intention, 140-143.

James, William, 48, 71, 75, 76, 82, 84, 91, 94, 99, 104, 116, 177.
Johnson, H., 238.
Jones, Sir Henry, 30, 248.
Jordan, D. S., 16.
Judgment, moral, 119, 127 ff., 136 ff.
  made by conscience, 109 ff.
  origin of, 128.
  relation to pleasure, 171-174.
  standard of, 127-138.
"Jukes," 24.
Justice, 207, 212-214, 218.

Kant, 159, 166, 191.
Kerschensteiner, 203.
Knowledge, 5, 59, 214, 218. *See also* Wisdom.

Laurie, S. S., 235.
Law, Moral, 79, 159-161.
  authority of, 162-164.
  of state, 127, 163, 223-224.
Lecky, W. E. H., 182.
Lloyd Morgan, C., 42, 56.
Locke, 34, 97.
Love, 78, 81, 82, 228-231.
Loveday, T., 66, 73.
Loyalty, 79, 190.
  to church, 244.
  to family, 229.
  to state, 227.
  to vocation, 194-199.

MacCunn, J., 157, 158.
M'Dougall, W., 45, 48, 56, 82, 111.
Mackenzie, J. S., 13, 66, 126, 152, 166, 179.
Marshall, A., 184.
Mediocrity, 19, 55.
Mercy, 213.
Metaphysics, vi., 199 n.
Mezes, S. E., 116, 219.
Mill, J. S., 111, 169, 170, 171, 179.

Money, 65, 189.
Monotony, 185, 197.
Montessori, M., 98, 99, 124.
Moore, G. E., 138.
Moral Education, Moral Judgment, etc. *See* Education, Judgment, etc.
Motive, 140 ff.
  test of right and wrong, 141 ff., 157.
Münsterberg, H., 202.
Muirhead, J. H., 13, 116, 126, 152, 166, 179, 248.

Nature, 38.
Nietzsche, 192.

Obligation, Moral, 123, 153, 164. *And see* Duty.
Opinion, private, 129.
  public, 131.
Opposition, 87, 106, 129.
Optimism, 246-248.

Pain, 167, 181.
Parental instinct, 47, 52.
Patriotism, 79, 81.
Pearson, K., 24.
Perseverance, 107, 184, 210, 217, 247.
Personality, 84, 89, 93, 241-242, 245.
  and vocation, 90-93, 242.
  education of, 97-99, 231.

Pittacus, 109.
Pleasure and happiness, 180-182.
  as moral standard, 171-174.
  as object of desire, 174-177.
  relation to the self, 177-179.
Precept, 33, 157, 230.
Progress, 89, 103, 126, 205, 209, 246-248.
  and instinct, 50.
  and variation, 20.

INDEX

Progress and vocation, 195.
Property, 224, 228.
Proverbs, 16, 115, 158.
Psychology, v. 41-116 *passim*, 202.
Pugnacity, 45, 48, 52, 54, 57.
Punishment, 145, 151.

Rashdall, H., 138, 204.
Reason as basis of moral judgment, 135 ff.
Reflection, 58, 59, 115, 214.
Reflex action, 43, 121.
Responsibility, 30-34, 38, 122, 123, 225, 245.
Right, 8-10, 89, 107, 114, 127-138, 139-145, 153-166, 171-177.
Rights, natural, 223.
  relative to duties, 227, 230.
Rousseau, 75.
Royce, J., 204.
Ruskin, 114.

Sadler, M. E., 9, 36.
Sanctions of Morality, 145-152.
  of Punishment, 145-147.
  of Success, 147 ff.
  Educational value of, 150-152.
School, 233-243.
  aim of, 201-203.
  instinctive basis of, 50-51.
  relation to conduct, 124-126.
  See also Education.
Scripture, 37, 81.
Seeley, J. R., 248.
Self, the moral, 83 ff., 193 ff.
  conflicts within, 93.
  growth of, 83-90.
  purposive, 100 ff.
  regulative, 100-102, 109 ff.
  relation to duty, 164-166.
  social nature of, 85 ff.
Self-abasement, 46, 49, 53.

Self-assertion, 46, 49, 53, 54, 191-196.
Self-control. *See* Temperance.
Self-preservation, 42, 56.
Self-sacrifice, 48, 105, 191-196, 228.
Selfishness, 169, 191, 229.
Sentiment, 77-82.
  education of, 80-82.
  variety of, 80.
Service, 244-248.
Seth, J., 179, 204.
Sex, instinct of, 46, 47, 54.
Shaftesbury, 111.
Shand, A. F., 66, 77, 79, 82.
Sidgwick, 178.
Socialism, 224-226.
Stability, Principle of, 18-19.
Standard. *See* Judgment.
State, 113, 120, 160, 166, 198, 222-227.
  instinctive basis of, 48, 51, 221.
Stephen, L., 111, 152.
Störring, 60.
Stoics, 62, 191.
Stout, G. F., 47, 56, 99, 104, 105, 106, 107, 116.
Suggestion in Education, 37, 39.
Sympathy, 88, 112, 133, 214, 229, 242.

Taylor, A. E., 116.
Teacher. *See* Education.
Temperance, 207, 211-212, 217.
Temptation, 31, 104, 211.
Ten Commandments, 132, 159, 163.
Thomson, J. A., 18, 22, 40.
Training, Moral, 235-241. *And see* Education.
Tufts, J. H., 13, 126, 152, 179, 204, 219.

Utilitarianism, 146, 169 ff.

Value, 2, 7, 123-126, 150-152.
   moral, 76, 89, 111, 123.
Value-for-life, 3, 4, 126.
Variation, 17, 19.
   acquired, 20.
   discontinuous, 20.
Vice, 32, 35.
Virtue, 35, 184, 205 ff.
   cardinal, 207 ff.
   in the school, 215-219.
   relative to vocation, 209.
Vocation, 5-7, 117, 166, 180-204, 227
   and ambition, 66.
   and personality, 90-93, 242.
   and virtue, 209.
   choice of, 182-191.
   loyalty to, 194-199.
   training for, 199-204.
Volition. *See* Will.

Voltaire, 7.

Weismann, A., 18.
Welton, J., 203, 233.
Westermarck, E., 111.
Will and character, 15, 100 ff.
   and decision, 105.
   and deliberation, 104.
   and desire, 102.
   and habit, 94 ff.
   and impulse, 60.
   and the self, 100-102.
   common, 220, 224, 228.
   training of, 105 ff.
Wisdom, 207, 214, 218.
Wish, 102, 103.
Whetham, W. C. D., and C. D., 232.
Wrong, 104, 115, 127-138, 139-152, 179.

BY
G. A. JOHNSTON, M.A., D.Phil.

Crown 8vo.   *8s. 6d. net.*

THE DEVELOPMENT
OF
BERKELEY'S PHILOSOPHY

EXTRACT FROM THE PREFACE

"No apology would seem to be required for an attempt to examine the historical development of Berkeley's Philosophy as a whole. There is no work in English or indeed in any other language which undertakes a critical examination of Berkeley's thought in its entirety. In this book I have tried to throw light on the evolution of Berkeley's thought by a careful study of his works in their chronological sequence and by detailed reference to his relations with his predecessors and contemporaries. I have naturally devoted most attention to what is central in Berkeley's philosophy—his metaphysics and Theory of knowledge,—but I have not neglected the other problems that were touched by his wide-roving mind."

LONDON: MACMILLAN AND CO., LTD.

Books for Students of Education

EXPOSITION AND ILLUSTRATION IN TEACHING. By Sir John Adams, LL.D. 6s.

THE EVOLUTION OF EDUCATIONAL THEORY. By Sir John Adams, LL.D. 12s. 6d. net.

THE DOCTRINES OF THE GREAT EDUCATORS. By Robert R. Rusk, M.A. 5s. net.

MACMILLAN'S TEACHING IN PRACTICE. An Encyclopaedia of Modern Methods of Teaching in the Primary School. Written by Recognised Authorities in Education and Edited by E. J. S. Lay. In 6 volumes, with a Portfolio of 172 Class Pictures. Sold in sets only. £6.

THE LOGICAL BASES OF EDUCATION. By Prof. J. Welton, M.A. 4s.

THE PSYCHOLOGY OF EDUCATION. By Prof. J. Welton, M.A. 10s. net.

THE TECHNIQUE OF EXAMINING CHILDREN. A QUEST FOR CAPACITY. By B. C. Wallis. 3s. 6d.

PRINCIPLES OF CLASS TEACHING. By J. J. Findlay, M.A. 6s.

SCHOOL MANAGEMENT AND METHODS OF INSTRUCTION, WITH SPECIAL REFERENCE TO ELEMENTARY SCHOOLS. By George Collar, B.Sc., and Charles W. Crook, B.Sc. 4s.

THE TEACHING OF SCIENTIFIC METHOD AND OTHER PAPERS ON EDUCATION. By Prof. H. E. Armstrong, LL.D. Second Edition. 7s. 6d. net.

SCHOOLS OF HELLAS. An Essay on the Practice and Theory of Ancient Greek Education, 600 to 300 B.C. By Kenneth J. Freeman. Edited by M. J. Rendall. With a Preface by A. W. Verrall, Litt.D. Third Edition. 7s. 6d. net.

A DEFENCE OF CLASSICAL EDUCATION. By Sir R. W. Livingstone. 6s. net.

LONDON : MACMILLAN AND CO., LTD.

Books for Students of Education

THE EDUCATIVE PROCESS. By W. C. BAGLEY. 7s. 6d.

CLASSROOM MANAGEMENT: ITS PRINCIPLES AND TECHNIQUE. By W. C. BAGLEY. 6s. 6d.

CRAFTSMANSHIP IN TEACHING. By W. C. BAGLEY. 6s. 6d.

EDUCATIONAL VALUES. By W. C. BAGLEY. 6s. 6d.

SCHOOL DISCIPLINE. By W. C. BAGLEY. 6s. 6d.

EDUCATION, CRIME AND SOCIAL PROGRESS. By W. C. BAGLEY. 5s.

AN INTRODUCTION TO TEACHING. By W. C. BAGLEY and J. A. H. KEITH. 7s. 6d.

THE STATE IN ITS RELATION TO EDUCATION. By SIR HENRY CRAIK, Bart. 2s. 6d. net.

SOURCE BOOK OF THE HISTORY OF EDUCATION FOR THE GREEK AND ROMAN PERIOD. By PROF. PAUL MONROE, Ph.D. 12s. 6d. net.

TEXT-BOOK IN THE HISTORY OF EDUCATION. By PROF. PAUL MONROE, Ph.D. 15s. net.

A BRIEF COURSE IN THE HISTORY OF EDUCATION. By PROF. PAUL MONROE, Ph.D. 10s.

PRINCIPLES OF SECONDARY EDUCATION. Written by a Number of Specialists. Edited by PROF. PAUL MONROE, Ph.D. 14s. net.

A CYCLOPEDIA OF EDUCATION. Edited by PROF. PAUL MONROE, Ph.D. In 3 vols. Illustrated. £3 3s. net.

LONDON : MACMILLAN AND CO., LTD.